HARNESSING THE UNICORN

To Larry Farlow,
alias all who inspire ordinary people to seek
and harness the unicorn of opportunity and thereby
to achieve extraordinary results.

Harnessing the Unicorn

How to create opportunity and manage risk

Pat O'Reilly

Gower

Published by
Gower Publishing Limited
Gower House
Croft Road
Aldershot
Hampshire GU11 3HR
England

Gower
Old Post Road
Brookfield
Vermont 05036
USA

Pat O'Reilly has asserted his right under the Copyright, Designs and Patents Act 1988 to be identified as the author of this work.

British Library Cataloguing in Publication Data
O'Reilly, Pat
    Harnessing the unicorn
    1. Creative ability   2. Creation (Literary, artistic, etc.)
    I. Title
    153.3'5

ISBN 0 566 07974 7

Library of Congress Cataloging-in-Publication Data
O'Reilly, Pat, 1943–
    Harnessing the unicorn / Pat O'Reilly,
        p.   cm.
    ISBN 0–566–07974–7
    I. Title.
PS3565.R387H37 1998
813'.54—dc21   98–5371
                                                                       CIP

Typeset in 11/14pt Times by Photoprint, Torquay, Devon
and printed in Great Britain at the University Press, Cambridge

Contents

v

Preface

Plato, Shakespeare, Mozart, Einstein . . . . That ordinary men and women should strive at all in the wake of such genius is in itself testimony to the optimism of Man. Yet ultimately a wake awaits the genius of every epoch, and, like mortar between these monolithic blocks, lesser intellects fill in the gaps of time. And somehow, not content with their minor roles, common people working together have made some uncommonly creative breakthroughs.

This book is about the *how* of creativity. But not the creativity of genius. It is about harnessing the creativity of ordinary people to achieve extraordinary results within a world that is full of risk and uncertainty. It is about the quest of one man – a man not blessed with any great intellect or talents – to harness the unicorn of opportunity. On his journey he is helped by the collective genius of his Fellow Man, personified herein as Larry Farlow.

Pat O'Reilly

Acknowledgements

My sincere thanks to Greg Whitear of British Aerospace and Bob Densley of BT for their perceptive criticisms of early drafts of the manuscript, and to Julia Scott who managed the project so professionally at Gower Publishing.

Chapter 1

In the beginning . . .

A daily diet of blame and shame for failed targets and missed deadlines; an irritating boss, irrational staff and irate customers; a backlog of jobs all of which were either emergencies, panics or crises: it was a hell of a mess. And I had dumped myself right in the middle of it.

I didn't want to let my customer down. I didn't want to let the company down. And to be honest I didn't want to let myself down by botching a job for the sake of a few more hours of hard graft. As a consequence, I was *always* overloaded: I hardly ever said 'no' to avoid overload, and when I did nobody took me seriously and invariably I ended up doing the work just the same.

You could say I was just unlucky. That's what I told myself. It's what I told Mary and the boys. Mary said she understood. I know the boys didn't – six-year-olds couldn't. Maybe Mary didn't either, but she made allowances. Perhaps she was all my good luck rolled into one. Mary was marvellous; the rest was hell.

Mind you, I wasn't alone: this hell on earth was incredibly

well populated. We created it all by ourselves, I and all the others – I know that now. But I escaped. That's why I'm writing this book: for the others who might never make it. For them, yes; but also for Larry as a sort of 'thank you'.

Larry was on the outside looking in. He understood. He showed me the way out. Well, that's not strictly true: I got myself into the mess and I, James Edward Hallam, eventually found my own way out of it. But it was Larry Farlow who convinced me there was a way out of that hell and into a better world, the world of opportunity – a part of creation that, for half a lifetime, I knew almost nothing about.

People who create and manage opportunities are rarely fazed by problems

Every thinking person gets to know about problems and risks. Cross the street without considering the risks from oncoming traffic and it's not long before you have problems. To some extent this book is about risk, but it is much more about opportunity. Both have something to do with uncertainty. Maybe that's why most people treat risks and opportunities in much the same way – as if opportunities are nothing more than risks with pleasantly acceptable outcomes.

Myth
Opportunities are simply risks with attractive outcomes

It's true, though: risks and opportunities do have a lot in common. Their timing, the likelihood of their occurring at all – these things are often difficult to predict. Some risks are unavoidable, just as some opportunities arrive simply by good luck. But I realise, now, that there are things we can do to reduce our exposure to risk. And there is no need to rely entirely on luck for opportunities, either.

You don't rely on luck to avoid unnecessary risks – Why leave it to chance to provide opportunities?

The consequences of a risk or an opportunity may be much smaller or greater than expected. Risks can turn into problems that cost time and money, wreck businesses, break up friendships, ruin careers, create misery, destroy lives. Opportunities, on the other hand, can help you get things done more quickly, at lower cost, or perhaps to a higher standard; they can also help build relationships, accelerate promotion, bring happiness, provide fulfilment.

So it might seem that risks come with minus signs in front of them and opportunities with plus signs – a nice simple concept.

Too simple! I know that now. Mind you, there was a time when I used to think of risks and opportunities in just this way. But that was before I met Larry.

Larry Farlow was a bachelor, and something of a recluse by all accounts. I knew that he was secretary of the chess club, and I'd heard that he played the flute pretty well. He had come down from our Rochester office and was now based with us.

Larry was a year or two younger than me – and, I soon discovered, a hell of a lot luckier. We had both held junior management positions in Consolidated Amsys, an international engineering company, for nearly five years. I worked on the communications side. We put in the monitoring systems in road tunnels; we set up links between off-shore islands and the mainland in developing countries – in fact we dealt with just about anything to do with communications. But really, of course, *we* didn't. We bought in most of the equipment, and generally we relied on local labour for much of the installation and commissioning work. Our direct contribution was small – and that was a problem for us: fluctuations in currency exchange rates could hack a big slice off our profits, delays always cost us dearly (and did we have problems getting things delivered on time!), and we made mistakes – who wouldn't in our position? We never became experts at anything.

But that was the job, and the variety was what had attracted me to it. In fact the other part of our work – the 'business as usual' part – wasn't anything like as interesting. We provided ongoing training and maintenance, often for ten years or more, on most of the systems we put in. It's where most of the profit came from. In fact it was thanks to the logistics team, as we called them, that our division had escaped the axe during the last reorganisation. Rumour was that it had been a close decision.

Larry's division served the transport market. I knew little about the work of that division except that it involved developing and installing systems for route scheduling, loading and vehicle maintenance. Latterly they had become involved with transatlantic haulage and shipping operations, and their roll-out programmes often involved bringing in major changes in two or three countries simultaneously.

For several decades the diversity of Amsys had been its strength: when one market was depressed, we could concentrate on others. Now our diversity was becoming our weakness. We were overstretched. We were up against people who specialised in what to us were our fringe markets. Start-up companies were able to challenge our established position. They could offer lower prices and greater flexibility. While we were telling our customer what was possible and what was not, they were saying 'yes' and then making the impossible possible.

We had an established track record, of course, but the trouble was that not all of our past was as glorious as we might perhaps have wished. The Communications division was a dinosaur in a rapidly changing environment. Gilbert Manning, the chief executive of Amsys, had recognised this and brought in new blood. (I had a new boss.) The trouble, as I saw it, was that it was more dinosaur blood.

In most businesses, managers at my level are pressured from all directions. Amsys was no exception. We had just come through our third restructuring exercise in seven years. Five divisions had been merged into three, and we had lost nearly 20 per cent of our staff, including two complete layers of management. Only one reporting layer remained between me and the main board of Amsys, and I now had three teams reporting to me – one on projects, one on logistics and customer support, and a third doing routine maintenance work.

The company had been turning in decent profit figures throughout the reorganisation, but in my division we were definitely losing market share – not quite what you would call free fall, but an uncomfortably rapid descent from market leadership in several of the sectors we served.

Things were more stable in the Transport and Business Services divisions, but there the pressure was on to increase market penetration to make up for the stagnation in Communications.

So one way and another, managers at the level of Larry and me felt most of the pressure. We had tough targets, inadequate budgets, tight deadlines, insufficient resources. I won't go on: there are plenty of jobs like that nowadays. Achieve more for less! None of this appeared to bother Larry Farlow. Things just seemed to *happen* for him, and he loved it. I dreaded happenings: they invariably *happened* to me.

Things just seem to happen for some people; they happen *to* others

I guess it was this that prompted the chief executive to cut Larry away from his division for a notional two days a week so that he could act as an internal process consultant. Basically, that's just a fancy name for someone who gets pulled in to trouble spots (or potential trouble spots) to give advice and help on things he knows nothing about. To be fair to Larry, from the beginning he admitted he wouldn't be able to contribute ideas on *what* we did, only on *how* we did it – on the management and communication processes we used.

Internal consultancy isn't a new concept, of course, but it was new to Amsys. Previously we had had to rely on expensive external consultants, and when we called them in we seemed to spend ages getting them to understand our business before they could do anything to help us. Now we had four people like Larry Farlow, two in the USA and two in Europe. They had gone through a pretty rigorous selection and training programme. (When I told Mary I was considering applying, she was horrified. "You mean try to sort out other people's work even though you can't manage your own?" She had a point. I'm not sure my track record would have stood up to probing questions. In any case Jean, my boss, had only been in her job a short while and there would have been nobody to take over from me during the ten-week training programme. So I decided not to apply, on grounds of my indispensability.)

The chief executive was responsible for more than two thousand staff in three operating divisions, but somehow he knew where all the serious problem areas were and he did try to provide help. Piling on the pressure wasn't Manning's style; I guess that's why we all looked up to him. In many ways Larry was rather like Gilbert Manning, but with more brains and a lot less charisma. People admired Manning for the person he was; they only got to appreciate Larry Farlow when they saw what he could do. He had a reputation, all right. Bionic Brain, someone had called him. Others (admittedly only those who had not worked with him) called him an arrogant pig; but never to his face. For some indefinable reason everyone tried to keep on the right side of Larry. It just seemed a very good idea not to cross him.

"How come you're hardly ever caught on the hop?" I asked him, the first time we got to talking about risk and opportunity. We were in my office – the temporary office I had moved into 'for a week or two' nine months earlier. (I've learned to beware of anything labelled 'temporary' in Amsys: there's nothing more permanent than a 'temporary measure' in our organisation.) "I mean, there must be plenty of risks in the work you have to manage. What's the secret?"

"There's no secret," he told me. "There are risks, true enough. But risk is only one side of the uncertainty equation. Most people seem to forget that on the other side there is opportunity."

Risk is only one side of the uncertainty equation. On the other side there is opportunity

"That's something I learned a long time ago," he continued. "Unless you are prepared to manage opportunity, the risks nearly always knock you off course."

Unless you manage opportunity, risks will nearly always knock you off course

"We're way off course most of the time here, Larry. But – *manage* opportunity? How do you mean?" I asked.

Larry stared at me thoughtfully. No, not *at* me, *through* me. He had that unsettling habit; I had heard others remark on it. There was nothing exceptional about him. He was shorter than average; stocky without being fat; but from his round face, topped by an untidy stack of prematurely greying hair, the bluest of eyes appeared always to be searching for the finest of details. You felt as though you were under a microscope.

"Tell me, Jim," he said. "What would happen if you were to ignore risks? Suppose you were to pretend they simply didn't exist. Would they go away?"

"No chance! It wouldn't be long before some of them became reality and gave me a thrashing. And that's my problem – they do. No matter how I try, I just don't seem able to foresee all of the risks in my work."

"Me neither," he admitted.

"So how do you manage? What do you do about it?" I asked.

"I just do my best. I keep reminding myself what I'm here for. I'm a manager, and if we already knew the best way of doing the job then almost certainly it wouldn't need managing. It might require supervising – maybe not even that. I have to manage the things that need managing, the things we don't do over and over again. What we're really talking about, of course, is managing change."

"Projects, you mean," I interrupted.

"Not necessarily," Larry replied. "Change in its most general sense. Difficult jobs, sometimes complex, always risky. The part of our work that is unique. But I don't just mean project work for our customers. There are plenty of internal assignments and change initiatives, too. You probably get your share of this sort of stuff, Jim. Assignments you take on for your boss, or perhaps just because *you* decide they are worth doing. Reorganising facilities, a special investigation, redesigning an existing process, setting up a new system, coaching a team member in a new skill. Anything that is being changed, or being done for the first time, involves risks."

Anything that involves change must involve risk

"Right," I said. These were just the sorts of things I was expected to fit in on top of the day job. It's OK until things start going wrong, which they never do one at a time – always all together. That's what turned an exciting, challenging job like mine into a high-pressure fire-fighting nightmare. "So you're saying risks are the main cause of my problems. Is that it?"

"Possibly," Larry said. "Although frankly I doubt it. But you could say that risks are a major source of opportunity. If there is little or no risk, it's likely there will be little or no opportunity."

Risks are a major source of opportunity

"Because that would mean we would have already done whatever it is at least once before, and successfully. Is that it?" I asked.

"Something like that," Larry replied vaguely. "But no one can foresee all possible risks. People forget things. They get careless and make mistakes. Accidents happen. Even with the best of risk-management plans there will still be the occasional crisis that makes your targets simply unattainable. You can't win them all."

Myth
Failure to meet targets is due to inadequate risk management

I couldn't really criticise my people. On balance, I had a pretty good team on the Bilston job. And unlike the youngsters looking after routine maintenance, and the old codgers in customer support, this team contained a good blend of youth and experience.

Jill was my unofficial second-in-command. Now in her late forties, she had worked for Amsys since leaving college and had been involved in projects around Europe and the Middle East. Pete was the hot-head of the team: technically brilliant, but inclined to take things personally. He had been very upset when we lost the follow-on order from the United Arab Emirates and he had to be switched to the Bilston bid. He complained a lot, but basically he was as keen as the rest of us to win the contract.

At twenty-three Nadia was the baby of the team. She had just graduated. The Bilston bid was her first real opportunity to prove her capability, and she was certainly putting in the hours. I would have liked to have had more time to help her: she was writing quite an important section of the proposal, and just how good her writing would be was as yet an unknown. I was not happy about this situation, but I had no choice: Bilstons had given us just two months to get the whole bid and proposal to them.

Dave was our anchorman. I was relying on his thoroughness and attention to detail to ensure that what we proposed to Bilstons would pass muster. The main problem with Dave was speed – or the lack of it. Everything he did was meticulous but it seemed to take for ever. Jean, on the other hand, thought Dave was mustard; the bee's knees. If I threw in the towel (I had seriously considered it after my most recent row with her), Jean would probably bypass Jill and promote Dave to head up the group.

Our track record in competing for work wasn't too bad. We won about a quarter of the contracts we bid for. But there the good news ended. We had lost money on three out of our last five contracts and that had led to the resignation of my previous boss, who had arbitrarily cut the price quotes to win the orders. But there is no doubt we would have done a lot better on those jobs if Lady Luck had been on our side. We also made mistakes; we had our share of accidents; and we spent a lot of time, effort and money on work that we had not planned on doing – stuff that was ignored or forgotten at the planning and estimating stage.

"We have all of those problems and more, Larry," I told him. "I could give you at least a dozen reasons why we fail to meet our targets. To be honest, actually *meeting* a deadline once in a while would be nice," I told him.

Larry grinned. "Life's a bitch, I know," he said. "But getting back to your present difficulties. What are you doing about the opportunities? They are your best bet for getting ahead of schedule, for driving costs down below budget."

Opportunities are the key to getting ahead of schedule and driving costs down

"How else are you going to gain the resource flexibility you need if you are to have any chance of dealing with setbacks you could *not* foresee?"

"Well – yes. Good point," I said, struggling to catch up with Larry's train of thought. This was certainly not the way I had become used to thinking about my job. "But how do you know there *are* opportunities in my sort of work?" I asked.

"That's an equally good point," he conceded. "I know next to nothing about the work of Communications division. But I'm pretty sure there must be opportunities for cost savings and short-cuts on most jobs, without sacrificing quality. And that's just for starters. There could be other kinds of opportunities, too – things you could do that would increase the *value* of your work without increasing the cost, for example."

I could see why some people thought Farlow was too arrogant to be a good consultant. Maybe that's why he stayed inside the company, where his track record was well known.

"So, are you suggesting that the reason I am overrunning the schedule and exceeding budget on most of my work is that I'm not managing these opportunities?" I asked.

"Well, are you?"

You dig yourself a deep hole; progress is painful; then you dive head first into the hole. That really hurts.

"I doubt it," I admitted ruefully. "I'm not sure I would know how to recognise an opportunity, as you call it. And I certainly haven't a clue how to manage one."

"Don't be so pessimistic, Jim. It's not complicated. Opportunities come in all shapes and sizes. There's no simple formula, although there are some useful guidelines. But you did say you take on some high-risk jobs, so at least you must be pretty good at recognising risks."

"Er, to be honest I'm not too sure about that either, Larry. In any case, what if our sort of work contains lots of risk and very little opportunity?"

Larry frowned. "I think that's rather unlikely," he said. "In my experience it's the high-risk things in life that contain the greatest opportunities."

The greater the risk in a job, the greater the opportunity

"Of course," he added, "if you don't recognise the opportunities or you don't know how to take advantage of them, then taking on any sort of high-risk work can be a dreadfully painful experience."

I nodded my agreement with the last bit. I hadn't been at all clever, judging by recent events. But I had to question the assumption that risk and opportunity are generally tied together. I asked what evidence he had for such a claim.

Larry didn't answer directly, but he asked me to list three innovations that had had a big impact upon people's lives. I came up with powered flight, television and the splitting of the atom.

"OK. And which of these would you say has opened the door to real opportunities?" he asked.

I thought about the many advantages of air travel. It's the only quick way of crossing oceans and continents. What a difference it has made to the everyday lives of globe-trotting business people and politicians, as well as to ordinary families taking their holidays. Air travel has made a world of difference.

And then what about television, that all-pervasive communication medium? It has spawned a huge industry. Education, entertainment, advertising, news broadcasting – life just isn't the same as it was before television.

But in many ways atomic power can also make a world of difference – quite literally, you might say. What about its effect on the course of the Second World War? And, despite what many people fear, the peaceful applications of nuclear energy are likely to be increasingly important in years to come, provided we can manage the safety issues properly.

"Well, they all did," I replied.

"OK," Larry said. "So plenty of opportunities have come from all of these innovations, and there are probably a lot more still to emerge. But did the pioneers have to take any risks?"

Larry had a point. They did, of course. We talked about the men who had lost their lives in those impossible flying machines. They must have realised they were dicing with death. But then what about the pioneers of television, striving for twenty years and more until at last their invention gave birth to a commercially viable product? The opportunities may have been great, but for those whose pet system was not adopted a lifetime's work was in vain. What a gamble! And then there were the atom researchers. The risks of playing around with nuclear energy are pretty obvious today, and even in those days I'll bet the scientists working on the A-bomb were only too aware of the huge gaps in their knowledge. Scary! How different the world might be now if the Western Allies had been runners-up in the atom race! When something goes wrong with a nuclear power station the repercussions are enormous, as Chernobyl proved. But in the longer term there must be tremendous environmental benefits if we can switch to safe, renewable energy sources.

"All right, but I'm still not convinced that risk and opportunity are linked and can *never* be separated," I said, "although I can see that they probably go hand-in-hand much of the time."

Larry frowned. "I can't *prove* what I'm saying," he said. "But I really do believe that if we can't see opportunity in a risky situation then either we have perceived unnecessary risks – risks that could and should be avoided – or we have failed to see or to create the opportunities inherent in that situation."

Where there is no opportunity, the risks are probably unnecessary

"Of course," Larry went on, "I accept that some risks are probably more imagined than real."

Some risks are more imagined than real

"Unique opportunities, on the other hand, are rather different. They have to be imagined before they can become real."

Unique opportunities have to be imagined before they can become real

"So now let me ask *you* something about risks and opportunities," he continued. "Remember what you said would happen if you were to ignore the risks in your work?"

"Yes. I said it wouldn't be long before some of the risks became reality. That's when life gets really interesting."

"By which you mean difficult? Unpleasant? Painful?" Larry asked.

"All three, and usually all at once," I told him.

Larry pressed on with the inquisition: "And how about opportunities? What do you think *they* do if you ignore them?"

"I don't see what you're driving at," I told him.

"OK, I'll tell you what happens. You are right about risks. They are the belligerent ones. If you try to ignore them they jump up and bite you. But opportunities aren't entirely passive, either – they're more the withdrawing type. Ignore them and they simply go away."

Ignore risks and they retaliate; ignore opportunities and they go away

"Yes, but . . ."

"Let's just settle for *yes*, Jim," Larry interrupted. "No buts. If you treat opportunities merely as if they were risks with good fortune attached to them, you are missing the greatest opportunity of all."

That was Larry. Typically obscure.

"All right," I said. "I give up. What *is* the greatest opportunity of all?"

"The opportunity to manage opportunity," he replied, heading for the door. "Think about it."

The biggest opportunity of all is the opportunity to manage opportunity

I thought about it. A lot. And I had to admit that Larry was right. Regardless of whether I was managing risk well or not so well, I was certainly doing nothing at all to manage opportunity. How many other people were in my position? Was the rest of humanity looking at the world the way Larry did? I doubted it. Was he a weirdo, or was the rest of the army out of step? But then, Larry was certainly successful, and I wanted to succeed. He was happy, and I was rapidly forgetting what happiness felt like. He had a good brain, and I used to think mine was OK, but in the last year or so I had begun losing confidence in mine. Or was it simply that Larry had time to use his brain?

Time. That was the difference. Larry had more *time* than I had. (Unless you were to count the nights I spent trying to sleep and failing, a tangled mass of problems writhing in my head.) He had time to think about things.

Productive thinking time: that's what *I* needed. Maybe then I could tie up a few of those loose ends and find time to manage opportunity. And maybe I could have a family life – something more than rushing home just in time to tuck the boys up in bed. And maybe even a social life again? A holiday without continual telephone harassment? Weekends without reams of paperwork? If managing opportunity could help me gain some time, then that's what I needed to do. And I've no doubt now that's why Larry called in to see me that afternoon. He had a single objective: to get me to start thinking about managing opportunity. Well, maybe that *was* the answer. If Larry Farlow could do it, why shouldn't I?

All this left me with one big question: How on earth do you manage opportunity? But maybe I could learn how – if I only had time.

That was when I decided to get myself a pocket notebook and to summarise my discussions with Larry Farlow as well as jotting down my own thoughts about managing risk and opportunity. Nothing complicated, just a few bullet points to serve as memory joggers.

I made a start.

Opportunity and risk: Beauty and the Beast

- Opportunities are much more than risks with pleasant outcomes.
- Without risk there is little or no opportunity.
- In general, the greater the risk, the greater the opportunity.
- Change is anything you have not done before or are doing in a new way; so, everyone has to manage change at some time.
- All changes contain risks; therefore, they are likely also to contain opportunities.
- Unless you manage opportunities, risks will invariably throw you off course.
- Where there is no opportunity, the risks are probably unnecessary.
- Some risks are more imagined than real.
- Unique opportunities have to be imagined before they can become real.
- Ignore risks and they retaliate.
- Ignore opportunities and they go away.
- The greatest opportunity of all is the opportunity to manage opportunity.

Action: I must find out how to manage opportunity.

Chapter 2

If I only had time

At the end of a week of disasters when my to-do list had grown from six lines to six pages and I had began to wonder whether keeping the list up to date wasn't a full-time job in itself, Larry Farlow called in to my office. It was five-thirty and he was on his way home.

"Still hard at it?" he gibed. "Never mind, at least you'll have the weekend to relax and forget all about work."

"Are you kidding? I've got two really urgent reports to get out by next Tuesday," I told him. "Either one is the better part of a weekend's work. The best I can hope for is to meet one of the deadlines. And that's assuming I can ignore everything else."

Larry's grin faded. "Surely your family need some of your time, at least at weekends," he said. "You can't just ignore them, can you?"

"Who's talking about ignoring the *family*? I meant if I ignore the other work. Next year's budget, for instance – I haven't even started thinking about that. And then there's the review of . . ."

Larry raised his hands, palms out, in front of my face. "Hold

17

on, Jim! You're not seriously suggesting you need to work weekends *as well as* staying late most weekday evenings."

"Well, no. Not *every* weekend," I replied.

Larry sat down on the corner of my desk. "Come on – the truth!" he urged. "How bad is it?"

"Most weekends," I admitted. "Right now it's pretty rotten, Larry. I've had a run of bad luck with one or two difficult jobs, and nothing I do seems to make a lot of difference. They just keep going wrong. I know what the problem is. It's the estimates. We cut them too fine. We always do. In the end we overspend our budget and eat into the profit margin."

"I see. You're in a pretty competitive market then?"

"No kidding!" I said. "But even at these prices we're struggling to win enough orders to keep the factory ticking over."

"Still, your prices must be pretty keen," Larry said. "So at least you should be popular with your customers."

"Er, not particularly. That's our other problem. We hardly ever complete a job on schedule."

"Oh. You mean, things take longer than you estimate *and* they cost more than you budget for?"

"Yes," I told him. "I guess the only thing we've got going for us right now is that when we do eventually finish a job our customer is usually pleased with the quality of our work."

"Good! Then at least there's hope. It means you're doing some of the right things well."

So far it had been a one-sided interrogation. I decided to turn the tables on my inquisitor: "Tell me, Larry. Do all of *your* projects go to plan, then?"

"Good grief, no! Not by any means. Most of them are OK, in so far as we're either on schedule or a bit ahead of what we promise. We do put a lot of emphasis on meeting our delivery promises. Our customers really value that. In the long run it saves us a fortune in sales and marketing costs, because customers keep coming back to us for more. But of course we have a few rogue jobs and they do take more than their fair share of management time. Inevitably these problem jobs overshoot budget, but that's something we have to live with. And we can, because the work we finish ahead of schedule nearly always turn in a bigger margin than we originally budgeted for."

Work finished ahead of schedule rarely exceeds budget

"It all sounds too good to be true, Larry. D'you mean you really can complete high-risk work on schedule?"

"Nearly always, yes," Larry said. "But there's no magic. We just plan the work and then work to make the right things happen. That's what management is all about."

"Ideally, yes," I agreed. "But I hear Transport division handles some pretty complex jobs. I mean – there must be plenty of unknowns in the work. You must get caught out *sometimes*."

"Sure there are unknowns. Like you, we're in the risk business and we have to manage those risks. We plan for things going wrong, and sure enough they do. Not always the things we expect, of course. And even when they are expected they sometimes find ways of going wrong that we had never imagined possible – often at times when we are least expecting it. But that's all part of the fun. We're learning new things all the while, including more about how to manage the uncertainties."

"OK. But we plan for risks, too," I told him. "Has anyone told you about the contingencies on the Bilston bid? That's the job I'm planning right now. The scary thing is that the risks are almost as big as the known work. If I let the engineers have their way the estimate would go through the roof and we would have no chance of winning the order. We really need to win this one, Larry. A lot of jobs depend on it."

Larry had stopped listening. He was busily poring over my cost estimates.

"Hey, I'm not sure I should let you see those . . ." I began. But I realised that the chief wouldn't have asked Larry Farlow to see me if he hadn't thought it was necessary. And in any case *I* wanted to know what Larry thought of our estimates; I wasn't entirely comfortable with them myself.

Larry looked up. "D'you want my opinion?" he asked.

I nodded, and he let the plans fall in an untidy heap on the desk.

"You'll probably win this contract, Jim," he said.

"Do you think so?" I asked, instinctively.

"Yes, I do," he replied, leaning back in the chair and staring at me coolly. "But I didn't come to that conclusion from reading the plan. I got it from reading your face. I reckon you intend carving chunks off the estimate until you get to what you think is the right answer. Am I right?"

"Of course not! Well – maybe. Sort of. But I've no choice but to cut the estimates. And before you start criticising let me tell *you* something. On the last four jobs we won, our price was never more than three per cent below our nearest competitor. We're pretty sure of that."

"All *that* really says is that your price was right," Larry said. "So maybe this new cost target of yours is about right, too. But you don't cut costs by cutting your price. How confident are you that you will be able to *meet* the target when it comes to doing the job?"

You don't cut costs by cutting your price

I was still in that hole, and I felt trapped. Larry had asked the very question that had been haunting me for a week or more.

"You know the answer to that one, Larry. I'm not at all confident. But as I see it I've got no choice. What else *can* I do?"

Larry got up and walked over to the window. He spoke with his back to me so that I had to strain to catch the words.

"It seems to me you have a choice," he said. "You could spend the next three days, including your weekend, on those reports. You *could* do that – or you *could* have a break, come back refreshed on Monday morning and rework the plans with your engineers so that you have a realistic chance of doing whatever it is Bilstons want you to do, on time, to your own high-quality standards, and at a cost that allows you a worthwhile profit margin."

"But what about my reports?" I asked.

He turned to me, a look of annoyance on his face.

"Who *needs* them? A *customer*?"

"In a way," I replied calmly. "An internal customer, actually – my boss, a divisional director. One is an urgent review of our furniture requirements for the next twelve months and the other is a survey of staff turnover figures. And before you ask me, the answer's yes. They're both needed urgently. The survey figures are for headquarters. They say its top priority."

"What would *they* want you to do well, those reports or this proposal for a major contract?"

"Both, of course. That's something I learned a long time ago. If a job's worth doing, it's worth doing well," I recited.

"That may *sound* all well and good," Larry replied with a deep sigh. "But do you really believe you can run a *business* that way?"

"It's a well-known fact," I told him.

"It's a well-known *myth*," he retorted.

Myth
If a job's worth doing, it's worth doing well

"If your director hasn't left for home, get him on the phone," Larry continued. "Say you can't finish the staff turnover reports on schedule *and* do a good job on the Bilston bid. Tell him you'll finish the report once the bid and the proposal document are completed. Go on, try it!"

I decided to call Larry's bluff. I phoned my boss, and had a hushed conversation with my back to Larry.

"Good night," I said loudly, and hung up.

"Well? What did he say?" Larry asked, returning to the chair by my desk.

"*She* – she said, 'That's fine!' " I replied, still rather shaken by Jean's answer. "D'you know, Larry, I'll never understand that woman as long as I live. Yesterday she said that report was top priority. *Top* priority. I assumed that meant more important than anything else I had on at the time. If people would only say what they mean and mean what they say, life would be a lot simpler."

"Thank goodness most people don't," Larry replied. "Customers asking for exactly what they needed? Suppliers promising only what they could actually deliver? Team members only saying 'I agree' when they had truly reached agreement? That *would* be scary. Who would need managers? You and I would be out of a job overnight. But think back, Jim. Has anyone ever given you an urgent job and said it was *low* priority?" I shook my head.

No one ever gives you an urgent job and says it is low priority

"No, I thought not," Larry continued. "Urgent, important and top priority sometimes get all tangled up and it's hard to separate them. But they're not necessarily one and the same thing, you know."

"I wish I did know," I said with a sigh.

"Tell you what. If you can spare the time, how about meeting to work out how you could save some time?"

"It's not that I'm ungrateful, Larry," I said. "I know you mean well, and you want to help. But it's all right for you. The old man has given you two clear days a week to do this sort of thing. And don't get me wrong, I think it's a good idea. But look at it from my point of view. Every hour I spend discussing ideas with you simply puts me another hour behind schedule. And that's my biggest problem. I need to save time. Everyone's got lots of ideas how I can spend more of my time on things *they* think are important."

If Larry had argued the point, I would have stormed off. But he didn't. He just looked me straight in the eye, nodded, and said: "You're right. It is easier for me to make the time than it is for you. So you decide. I'll call in Monday lunch-time in any case. I'll be interested to know how your weekend went."

I went home without a bulging briefcase, and I enjoyed the weekend break. But when Larry called in at lunch-time on Monday I was up to my eyes in paperwork. The engineers had gone right through the figures again, and I now had to get the whole lot into some sort of shape ready for costing. And I still had those two reports to do. And I hadn't yet checked my in-tray – there was bound to be loads of new stuff in the mail. (There always is when you're overloaded.) And my e-mail . . .

"I'm sorry, Larry, I really can't . . ."

Larry held up a hand to silence me. "Don't tell me," he said. "You're too busy. You can't spare the time to hear about ideas to help you save time."

Put like that my objection did sound ridiculous. I cleared my desk and locked away the papers.

"You're right," I said. "Let's go."

Over lunch, Larry put to me a modified version of the principle I had been lauding three days earlier: "Any job that's worth doing needs to be done adequately. But not necessarily as well as you possibly can."

If a job's worth doing at all, it's worth doing well enough

"The operative word is *adequately*," he went on. "Anything more is a waste of time, and therefore a waste of opportunity. The enemy is perfectionism. It's deeply ingrained in the nature of many of us to put our very best into everything we do. But perfection in everything is quite unaffordable."

Perfection in everything is quite unaffordable

I could feel myself frowning. I was no saint but I did take a pride in my work, and the idea of intentionally churning out second-rate stuff made me feel very uneasy. It happened all too often, of course: things went wrong despite all my efforts to do my best.

"Let me ask you this," Larry continued. "How much will it improve your chances of winning the Bilston contract if you produce a really good report on your department's furniture requirements?"

I said nothing. What could I say?

"OK. So do you know what furniture you need?" Larry asked.

I nodded. "A couple of desks and chairs for the new people who are joining us in October. *If* we win the Bilston job, that is. And we're really desperate for filing cabinets. Oh, and Jill says a plan-file cabinet would help us keep our large drawings tidy. The place always looks a mess with rolls of yellowing prints gathering dust on top of every cupboard, and it'll be at least a year before we can get it all into the computer archiving system."

Larry tore a page from his pocketbook.

"*Jean*. Is that right?"

I nodded, and Larry scribbled:

Dear Jean

About next year's furniture requirements: My department needs two new desks and chairs, and three or four filing cabinets. And if there's any money left in the kitty, a plan-file cabinet would help us keep the place looking tidy.

"There! All *you* have to do is sign it and your report is finished," he said.

"You must be joking," I told him. "A proper report would have to show floor layouts and say who is going to use each item. It would need to list the existing furniture and show that it is all being fully utilised. And I always think it's helpful to include . . ."

"Stop! I'm sure you're right, Jim. But is writing a *proper* report the proper thing to do?"

I frowned.

Larry sighed.

"You're not with me, are you?" he asked. I shook my head and he continued: "Right. Then would an example help?" I nodded, and he went on: "OK. Well, my friend Sue is a freelance writer. She does her tax returns just well enough to stay out of prison. Hardly spends any time at all on admin. But her writing is brilliant. It's well planned, stylish, and always thoroughly checked and professionally presented. And never, ever late. She is widely respected by her clients. Needless to say, Sue has always got plenty of work."

"But the tax inspector is her customer, too," I complained.

"Maybe. But do you really believe that stylish tax returns and rushed copy would be a recipe for success?" Larry asked.

Perfection is the thief of excellence

"No. All right, I take your point," I said.

"Good! But try *using* it," Larry urged. "It works. Trust me."

It was not without apprehension that I presented Jean with the hand-written memo about our furniture needs.

"Is this *it?*" She asked. "It's not up to your usual standard, Jim. A bit light on detail – oh, I know what I wanted to ask you. Gilbert was quizzing me on how things are going with our proposal for Bilstons. We won't have to go begging for an extension to the closing date on this one, will we?"

"I'm pretty sure that won't be necessary," I told her. "Everything's under control. We're working on the plans and costings at the moment, and the proposal seems to be taking shape at last."

"Great! I'll want some time with you to go through the estimates," Jean said, breaking into one of her rare smiles. "Oh, and about those staff-turnover figures. I'll tell Jack Parton we are too busy on the Bilston bid. I'm sure I can get him to settle for global figures for the whole division. If necessary I'll refer him to Central Records."

"You mean – I don't have to bother with the report? It wasn't really all that important?"

"Well, not *that* important," Jean replied. "I mean – all things are relative."

"What's that supposed to mean?" I asked, irritably. "I nearly wrote up that report this weekend. I might have given up most of my weekend for something you now say was *not all that important*! It would help me a lot, Jean, if you would tell me when jobs aren't really important."

"How can you *nearly* write a report? Anyway, there's no need to guess. You can always *ask*, you know."

Ask! Now why didn't *I* think of that? Another powerful management technique! It seemed that experts were queuing up to educate me in the blindingly obvious. I decided to discuss this at the next session with my new-found friendly guru, Larry Farlow. He would surely have a view on this.

When you're unsure of priorities, it is not cheating to ask

"Of course! Why not?" Larry agreed. "If you're uncertain about priorities, you can always ask. But you really ought to consider the alternatives. On some parts of your work you can save a lot of time by purposely doing things badly. Just so long as badly is good enough. And there is always the possibility that if you do an unimportant job badly enough you won't ever get asked again."

Larry's eyes twinkled mischievously, but I could see the sense in what he was saying. Even so, I had to put up a token resistance. "What if you get it wrong?" I asked. "I mean, supposing the perfectionist is right and the job really does need doing very well. What then?"

"Then you will have made an error of judgement," he replied. "There's always that risk, of course, and that's where asking comes in. Remember, though, that it's often worth getting a second opinion if you are given a high-priority job by a perfectionist. Doing the job *well enough* could mean doing it as well as you are able to, or it could mean not even bothering to do it at all. Saving time when it is right to save time will give you more time to do the important things really well. Important things like managing opportunity."

That was when the simple truth dawned on me: asking for more information is simply a way of reducing the risk of misinterpreting the priority of a job. Proactive risk management.

Asking for more information is a proactive risk-management technique

I put it that way to Larry, and he agreed. "Exactly! Information can be powerful stuff, and dangerous if mishandled. Information management is important in risk management – as it is in opportunity management, too."

"It is? I'm sorry, you've lost me there completely. Where does opportunity come into it?"

Larry smiled. "To see how that works we really need to look at the proactive part of your time management. So far, we have only been talking about your reactive management. How you respond when you are up against tight deadlines, for example."

"To be honest, Larry," I said, "that's pretty well how things are most of the time here. We only have enough time to work on the urgent jobs. Except, of course, when we get distracted by crises or diverted by screaming panics. So much goes wrong nowadays that planning anything seems a total waste of time. I sometimes feel guilty when I spend time planning. But not often, because I don't do a lot of planning any more."

"That's no solution. In fact it could even be your biggest problem. There's nothing proactive about crisis management. It's entirely reactive. The storm troopers may feel that they're doing a great job as they battle to salvage something from a ghastly situation, but in most cases they are the very people whose lack of planning causes the problems in the first place."

"I know the types," I agreed. "We hand pick them for my department. They're the only ones who can stand the pressure."

"Maybe," Larry said. "But the trouble for most of us is that when we are up against impossible deadlines we rarely perform at our best. When there's no time to think things through, we tend to make poor decisions. Or, worse still, to waver indecisively until we have no options. And even if something worthwhile is salvaged at the end of it all, we are often too emotionally drained to feel any real sense of achievement."

I could identify with all of that – not that it made me feel any better to look at my open sores through a microscope. I remembered the chaos when Ransom and Fellowes, who were supplying us with purpose-built stabilisers for an off-shore microwave link for one of our Gulf state customers, had a factory fire. The fire could have been a lot worse: R&F were back in production within four months. But we had no disaster-recovery plans whatsoever. We survived that one by re-scheduling the whole programme and working around the clock for three months once the stabilisers became available. I saw Mary and the boys for just five Sundays that summer. (On two of them it rained.) In the end, I insisted they went on holiday without me. (Mary was for cancelling the trip.) And then, when young Stephen was taken ill, Mary and Andrew spent three days of the holiday at the hospital. Things were a little strained between us for some time after that.

It wasn't just me: the whole team suffered because of our lack of contingency planning, and you might have thought we would have learned from that experience. But no. Within a couple of months we were into late-night working once again, and I felt really depressed. By putting in the hours I could just about keep on top of things at work, but I would come home and find notes from Mary, such as: '*Called the Johnsons at 7 pm when you weren't back. Told them we couldn't make it to their B-B-Q. The boys were disappointed so I've taken them for a swim. See you later – if you are in.*'

And I'd forgotten all about the barbecue.

"True enough, Larry," I agreed. "And you think proactive time management is the answer?"

"Proactive *management*, yes. Of time, certainly. But also of resources, of risks, of opportunities."

"There you go again – opportunities. What *is* this opportunity management thing you keep rattling on about, and what the hell has it got to do with time management?" I asked.

Larry launched into another of his monologues. He told me that good time management is very much more than bring-forward files and to-do lists. Proactive time management creates the foundation for opportunity management, and that in turn is the basis of sound business management and sensible career management. He even suggested that proactive opportunity management is a philosophy of life, but I decided to let that hare run without giving chase.

Proactive time management is the foundation of opportunity management

I was still far from convinced that any of this could work in the high-pressure environment I had to operate in. I told him as much. I said I couldn't see any real link between opportunity management and time management, except that if you run out of time you can't manage *anything* properly.

Larry sketched out what at first glance appeared to be a fairly traditional time-management priority chart, where all the things that need doing can be fitted somewhere on a grid, depending on their importance and their urgency.

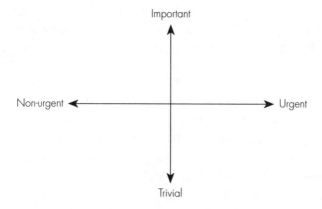

But then he got the priorities all wrong:

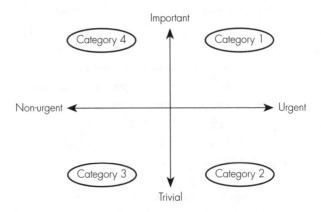

I told him this was a load of nonsense. I couldn't see why jobs that are trivial but urgent should be given higher priority than important but non-urgent jobs. And come to that, why should I devote any time at all to jobs that are trivial and not even urgent?

"I thought we had already sorted out the category twos," he replied. "Remember the furniture report? You produced it on schedule, but you reacted to its relative unimportance by doing the minimum you could get away with, and so you saved yourself a lot of time. Unless you can sleep faster this is just about the only way to free up the time you say you need."

I made no comment, and Larry continued. "If you ignore the category twos you'll get no peace to concentrate on anything else. People will just keep interrupting you with such mind-numbing stuff as 'Have you got me those cost estimates for the paper plates and party hats for Open Day?' I assume you get your share of that sort of junk work?"

"Yes, lots of it," I told him. (In the past two years I must have organised at least a dozen VIP visits and tours of the factory – not to mention the Annual Management Conference, which had suddenly become my baby after I criticised the lack of organisation when Chris Delaney was running it. And any site reorganisation invariably got dumped on my desk. These special assignments probably cost me at least a day per week – and a long day at that.) "I do nothing else some days. All right, Larry. Maybe there is some logic in polishing off category two jobs quickly and without gilding the lily. But surely not just so that I can waste time on non-urgent trivia. What about the category threes on your chart? Now there's a load of nonsense if ever I saw one."

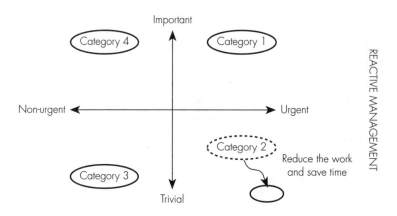

"That's right," he said. "It does seem like nonsense. I wouldn't mind betting that lots of people spend time on category three jobs just *because* it doesn't matter whether they do them well or not. It's not real work. It's more like playing. And, let's face it, most people get very little fun out of their work, so playing around with a few category three jobs is a welcome relief from the pressures of their normal work."

"Marvellous!" I said, sarcastically. "So after showing me how to save valuable time, you're now suggesting that I should waste it on all sorts of trivia that aren't even urgent. I'm sorry, Larry, but I really can't see the logic of that."

"You're right. Or you would be but for one thing. Watch this," he said. And then he added another arrow to his sketch:

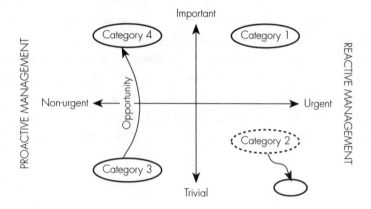

"To make sense of it," he continued, "you have to move some of the category threes up into the top left-hand quadrant. In other words, you increase their importance. And of course" – here he sketched yet another arrowed line from category four down to category three – "to make room for them you will almost certainly have to move some of the category fours down into what was the category three box, where they become less serious."

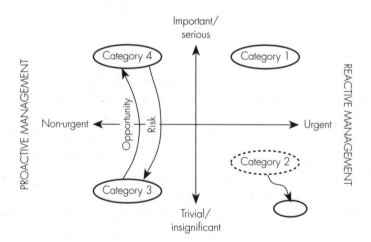

"I see. So you're saying make the things I want to do more important and make the things I don't like doing less so. In other words you're suggesting I should give higher priority to important jobs, but at the same time *I* should decide what is important. Is that it?"

Larry nodded. "Yes, basically," he agreed.

"It looks simple enough on paper, Larry," I told him. "And I've no doubt that you've got some magic way of doing this. But my problem is that the sorts of jobs I get given have their priorities set by other people – by my director or by our customers, for example – and there's not a lot I can do about it."

"Not if you're only managing reactively, you can't. Not if you wait until everything becomes a crisis. Right now, other people may set many of the priorities on your objectives. They decide what you have to *achieve*. But it's still up to you to decide what you *do*, and you *can* prioritise the activities that take up your time. In other words, even if you haven't set your own priorities in terms of objectives you can still determine how best to achieve them."

I could see that he had a point. I nodded, and he continued: "Better still, why not take control right from the start? Really effective time management is impossible if you always adopt other people's priorities on what you must achieve and their views on how to go about it."

Effective time management is impossible if you always adopt other people's priorities

"Effective management is much more about getting others to accept and support some of *your* priorities. In other words, it's about being proactive – that's management speak for taking the initiative."

Proactive management is about getting others to accept and support some of your priorities

It didn't make much sense to me, but I already knew Larry Farlow well enough to be sure that he was being serious.

"Let's see if I understand what you are saying," I said. "You're telling me that, provided I give time to them early enough, I really *can* make some of the important things less important, and vice versa. Is that it?"

"That's right. Reducing the importance or the seriousness – for example, changing a situation so that you reduce the consequences of getting things wrong or the chance of mistakes occurring – is the essence of proactive risk management."

"I see," I replied. "So, let me guess. Raising the benefits that come from doing something well, and increasing the chances of success – is that what you would call proactive opportunity management?"

Larry beamed. "You've got the idea," he said. "That's not the whole of it by any means, but it's a pretty good start."

I shook my head. "I'm glad to know that *you're* pleased, Larry. But there's just one problem. Well, two actually. How . . ."

"Don't tell me. Let *me* guess, this time," Larry interjected. "How to shift some things upwards? And how to shift other things downwards?"

"Right on both counts," I confirmed.

"Left, actually," Larry replied, obscurely. "As a rule you will find it very much easier to raise or lower the priority of things that are on the *left* of the diagram. Once things have drifted across to the right-hand side and become urgent, as in time they all tend to, you are forced to operate in reactive mode and you rarely have much flexibility. What we're talking about is *proactive* management of risks and opportunities. Proactive risk management is a logical process, and most people find it relatively easy – at least to understand, if not always to apply. In my division, we use the technique on all our work. It makes life a lot easier for us."

**Proactive risk management is a
logical process, simple to
understand if not always easy to
apply**

"Proactive opportunity management, on the other hand, is something quite different," he said. "It's a creative process. It hardly ever seems to make sense. Except afterwards, of course – once someone has done it."

Proactive opportunity management hardly ever makes sense – until someone does it

I asked Larry to show me how it was done, but he seemed a bit cagey. He muttered something about everyone having to find their own unicorns. I found that particularly unhelpful, and I told him so. In the end I did get him to promise to dig out a few case studies on opportunity management. Like many people, I learn more quickly from examples than from discussing abstract concepts. I still felt that Larry was hiding something from me. But why?

Anyway, I had spent quite enough time talking about how to save time. There was work to do. But first, while they were still fresh in my mind, I jotted down a few key points from our discussion; these I would transfer to my opportunity-management notebook that evening.

Making time for opportunity management

- If a job is worth doing, it's worth doing *well enough*; anything more is a waste of time and, therefore, a waste of opportunity.
- Perfection is the thief of Excellence.
- Asking for more information is a proactive risk-management technique.
- Proactive time management is the foundation of effective opportunity management.
- Proactive management of risks and opportunities can reduce the cost of failures and increase the value of successes.
- The cost of an activity can often be reduced or the benefits increased – provided you take initiatives early enough.
- There is usually little opportunity for improving the cost-effectiveness of work done in a panic.
- Effective time management is impossible if you always adopt other people's priorities.
- Proactive management is about getting others to accept and support some of your priorities.
- Proactive opportunity management hardly ever makes sense – until sombody has done it.

Action: I need to find out more about different types of opportunities and how this idea of proactive opportunity management works.

Chapter 3

The unicorn: a natural beauty

That working lunch took more than the hour I had budgeted, and I hurried back to the department hoping to see Jean Cartwright before she got engrossed in her afternoon's work. I didn't get that far.

John Scriven, a member of my Customer Support team, met me at the door. His usually cheerful face was set in a frown.

"Sorry, Jim. I know you're busy, but there's trouble. Can you help?"

Trouble? There was *never* trouble with Customer Support. I banked on it running smoothly. I hardly ever got involved. I talked to John before he did the staff appraisals, and we got together once every six months to look at budgets. But other than that I signed off their monthly reports and that was all there was to it. And trouble I did not need; not right now. Not while we were in the middle of the Bilston bid.

"It's Cantwells," he said. "They're complaining that we're holding them up for spares. But I've checked, and their buyer got the part numbers wrong on their last order, and so nothing got through to Shipping. It's not our fault."

"You're sure?" I asked.

"Positive. But they say they're writing to Gilbert Manning about it. They're blaming us."

"So what have you done?"

"Well, straight away I faxed them a copy of their order. It clearly shows *they* got the part numbers wrong. But they weren't satisfied. They asked to talk to you, but you weren't in."

"Blast!" I said. "OK, let me have all the relevant paperwork and leave it with me. I'll prepare a brief for the chief exec. He's not going to like this."

If we had had a decent computer system for spares handling this sort of thing would never have happened. But I also thought maybe I needed to organise some sort of training for the Customer Support team. They had never had any training, and I only had John's word for it that it wasn't their mistake. (I put chalk on the snooker cue after every bad miss!)

When I had put the brief together and phoned the chief executive's office, I was told he was away on business, so I had no option but to call Cantwells and deal with the matter myself. Their buyer was in a really bad mood. It sounded as though he had been on the receiving end of some rough treatment from his own people, too. To placate him, I agreed to get a small batch of spares together and get them delivered by courier the next day.

"Your chap was trying to blame *me*," the buyer said. "It's *our* job that has been held up for over a month. What you people at Amsys don't seem to realise is that we have to deal with dozens of orders every day. Your customer support people should have told us straight away that the part number and description didn't line up. As it is, we're in a tight corner and all I get from Amsys is *'It's not our fault'*. I'm not interested in excuses. I want customer *service*. That's what we pay for."

"Good point," I said, weakly. "Look – leave it with me. I'll make sure we get the first batch of spares to you by tomorrow. And there won't be a surcharge for courier service, of course."

That last bit was a mistake.

"I should think *not*!" he said, and the line went dead.

It was mid afternoon by the time I had sorted out the Cantwell problem, and I still needed to see Jean Cartwright. I couldn't help wondering how she would take my conversion to this new faith, the pursuit of opportunity. I wanted to bring her into the network right from the start. I felt I ought to. But she wasn't the most approachable of people and it might be better to get my own ideas straight first. One thing was certain: she would ask questions – questions I probably couldn't answer, not yet at least. And one thing I had learned about Jean: she did not like unanswered questions. Would she use that as an excuse to reject the whole thing?

Jean Cartwright was in her mid-forties and had been head-hunted from a large multinational. She had been my boss for little more than three months. I suppose I resented her appointment, perhaps irrationally. If things hadn't gone so badly on the United Arab Emirates contract I might have been in the frame for promotion, although I'm not sure I was ready for it in any case. I could hardly blame Gilbert Manning for passing me over: he had published the requirements – proven track record of profitable, on-time completion of projects; proven ability to deliver support services to a consistently high standard. These were just the very aspects of my recent past I was struggling to live down. Now if he had been looking for willingness to work long hours, proven ability as a crisis manager, then maybe I would have been a strong applicant, whereas Jean Cartwright had the qualifications, the experience (ten more years than I had) and a track record of success. Any grounds for resentment on my part were imaginary, but the disagreements we had (and there were plenty) were real enough.

What really got to me was the way she tried to tell me how to do my job. *What* to do – fine: she was my boss. But not *how*. Although she knew the communication systems industry pretty well, she had almost no experience of our market sectors and of the way things worked in Amsys. While Jean was still finding her feet, she was over-anxious to make her mark. (I bore the scars of her first attempts.)

But there was more to it than that. We just didn't gel: it was a classic personality clash. Jean was what you might call a fine-line person; I'm more the broad-brush type. The way I saw it, she had no real need to understand all of the details herself; she only needed to make sure there was someone in the group who did. Inevitably, Jean saw things differently. She wanted all the details. Everything. She was the archetypal perfectionist. Already this had caused me no end of grief. Fortunately, we shared two important objectives: we both wanted the business to succeed and we both wanted our customers to be happy with the service we gave them. This may well have been all that prevented things getting out of hand between us, because we disagreed on just about everything else – certainly on how to achieve these objectives and what our priorities should be.

Jean was a neat and orderly sort of person, always smartly dressed and with her hair in a tight bun with no loose ends. She kept her lips shut tight until she had something to say, and then she was straight to the point, following up with the detail – all of it that was relevant and necessary – in a neat and orderly, talking textbook kind of way. And then she would shut up. To be fair to her, it was efficient: she said things only once. Having thought carefully before saying anything (I found her precipitous pauses really disconcerting), Jean expected people to understand her. It seemed to come as a shock, a real disappointment, if ever you asked her a question. It was as if she saw it as a failing on her part for not providing just the information that was needed exactly when you needed it. Yes, she liked things to be complete. Neat, complete and concise: that would do as her epitaph. (On second thoughts, no need for the 'and'.) Her work was always neat and concise; the trouble was, she expected everyone else to work that way. She lived by systems, by rules and procedures, by checklists and performance measures. She hated loose ends.

As a business strategist Jean had analytical abilities that were way above my own; I will admit that. But as a manager of people she had a massive blind spot. She suffered from chronic motivation blindness. Her entire world consisted of numbers and facts. (People were numbers.) What she saw was what you got: a score out of ten. I got very few. It would have been nice to have got some small word of encouragement once in a while, but I knew better than to expect it.

Jean's reaction to these radical ideas of Larry's was predictable. No red-faced impatience as I unfolded the time-management cum risk-management cum opportunity-management philosophy. No wringing of hands, no raising of eyebrows, no tapping of feet. But I knew. From the metallic edge to her voice, from the measured pauses before and after each carefully chosen adjective, I knew she remained unimpressed.

"And how much management effort do you intend devoting to this – new faith? How much time can you spare for philosophising on the – imaginary future you would like to make happen if only you had" – a double pause before she spat out the last two words – "*more* time?"

"Listen, Jean," I retorted. "If someone is willing to help me to get better results, why should you worry? Anyway, you know that Gilbert Manning is backing what Larry does in this company. And mostly it's my own time I'm spending trying to improve this division's performance. Don't you think you could be a bit more supportive?"

"I'm telling you how *not* to waste your time," she said. "That *is* being supportive. It's my job to support improved performance. And it's your job to perform. That's why I spent so much of my time preparing for your appraisal last month. That's why I set targets for improving your efficiency. Remember?"

Jean still saw staff appraisals as something you did to your staff. But this was not the time to push my own views on that hoary old chestnut. I tried another tack.

"Hang on, Jean," I said. "We shouldn't be too pedantic about targets. It's overall results that matter, and with Larry's help I'm beginning to see how we can improve our results. In any case, if I get some things done more quickly wouldn't you call that an improvement in efficiency?"

"Only if they're done well. A botched job might be good enough for you, Jim, but you should have noticed by now that I'm not easily fobbed off with mediocrity. And don't forget – you work for *me*. And in part at least *I'm* judged by the quality of *your* work!"

"I may *report* to you," I retorted, "but I *work* for our *customers*. And so do you, I hope."

"All right. *Now* who's being pedantic? Anyway, I haven't got time to waste on semantics. I agree that we both need to put our customers first when it comes to setting priorities. And I do. Did I make a fuss about that pathetic report of yours on furniture requirements?"

"No, I guess not," I conceded. (In arguments with Jean Cartwright you sometimes felt she had had the last word before you could get in with your first.) "I'm sorry. But Larry Farlow really has set me thinking. And I'm thinking there could be a lot to gain by improving our approach to risk management. I'd like to get Larry on board for the Bilston bid, if not to help with the work at least to give us a second opinion. In any case, Bilstons are insisting on seeing a risk-management plan, so it had better be good."

"That's fine by me," Jean said. "By all means use Farlow if you think it will help. Just so long as it doesn't hold things up. I may be new to Amsys, but I'm not as green as all that. I do know that Bilstons are seen as market leaders for their tender-vetting procedures. They get it right. If Bilstons accept your bid you really *are* the best."

"That's not how they're viewed here, Jean," I told her. "Bilstons are bureaucrats. They nit-pick over every little detail, they screw you right down on price, and they take so long to make a buying decision that you're half-way through the delivery timescale before you get a contract. And even then they expect you to meet the original target dates."

Jean was shaking her head before I had finished.

"They only nit-pick, as you call it, when they get incomplete or incoherent proposals. And you can't blame them for applying sound cost-control measures to their procurement. Bought-in goods and services probably account for over 80 per cent of their costs. And as for expecting suppliers to deliver on time – what's wrong with that?"

I couldn't believe I was hearing this.

"You're supposed to be on *our* side," I said. "If you think Bilstons are doing everything right, why didn't you join them instead of Amsys?"

"As a matter of fact, I did consider it. They made me a very good offer, but I decided to come here precisely because Bilstons didn't need me and Amsys do. Bilstons meet their targets, and Amsys do not. Or did not. From now on we're going to. So remember – we've *got* to meet the deadline for this bid. If we can't even deliver the proposal on time, what message will that convey about our ability to hold to their upgrade schedule?"

"Point taken," I agreed. "But most particularly, Jean, I really do want us to look into this idea of opportunity management. It will take time, but I'm convinced it will be worth the effort."

"Fine, Jim. If it means that much to you, you go right ahead. But not until you've put the Bilston proposal to bed. I don't want anything to divert your attention from this one. And that's final."

"If you say so," I conceded, accepting that the audience was nearing a close if not a conclusion. "But I think you ought to know what Larry thinks. He has a hunch we're going to need an opportunity-management plan if we're to have any chance of making a profit on the Bilston deal. I assume you're happy for me to look into opportunity management in my *own* time? Until either I'm convinced that Larry is talking nonsense or I can convince you that he's talking sense."

Jean shook her head. "No way am I going to base the running of this division on the wild hunches of Larry Farlow. Or anyone else. How you spend your spare time is your business. But quite frankly, Jim, I'd have thought you had more than enough to do for the next few weeks without setting off on a tangent."

Jean's phone rang (prearranged?) and I had to leave without pressing the matter further, which was just as well because I was pretty mad. But far from denting my resolve, her head-in-the-sand response only made me more determined to press on with my investigation into opportunity and how to manage it.

"Did you remember the case studies?" I asked Larry when we met after work later that week.

"I did, actually," he replied. "But before we look at how other people have made use of opportunity management it might be worth talking about opportunities in general. They're not all the same, you know. There are several species."

"How do you mean?" I asked.

"Well, you can think of them as falling into at least four distinct categories."

"Based upon the level of benefit and the degree of urgency?" I asked hopefully.

"Hm, interesting idea. You could do, I guess. My way is to group them according to what it is that you have to do."

"I don't see what you're driving at," I told him.

"Well, look at it this way," Larry replied. "There are at least four basic types of opportunities. The first of these are obvious, because other people have already exploited them. But, for a time at least, they can still provide benefits to those who follow the leaders. The real advantage is only there for the trail blazers, of course. They get the biggest benefits."

"For example?" I pressed.

"OK – what about the forty-niners? You know, prospectors in the gold rush. Those who joined in early enough did pretty well out of the bonanza, but as time went by so the rich pickings gave way to much poorer ones. The stragglers had a lean time – panning for gold, finding next to none; living in forlorn hope, dying in abject despair. They couldn't see it, of course, but the opportunity had passed them by."

I could see what he meant. I nodded, and Larry went on to describe three more kinds of opportunities. Some are windfalls that arrive without you doing anything, and the challenge is to recognise them before they can get away. Then there is a third type: hidden opportunities that you have to go out and hunt for.

And finally – and, he suggested, quite often these are the ones with the greatest payoff – there are opportunities that you can create.

"Four distinct species, then," I remarked. "I had never thought of it like that before. I suppose the first group could be called copycats. Learning from what others have done before."

"That's right," Larry replied. "Only fools learn everything the hard way. Keeping an eye open for other people's innovations is unlikely to make you world-class, but it's a pretty good way of keeping up with the pack until you can find your own means of getting ahead. Plenty of businesses chug along quite nicely for years just by cloning the products of market leaders. Of course, they are hardly likely to enjoy the profit margins of the real innovators. The personal computer market is a good example. It's just a matter of being receptive to new ideas and avoiding the 'not invented here' syndrome. Sometimes the innovator is not so good at implementing, and then someone else can step in and take the cream off the benefits cake. Another ploy is to take an innovation from one business sector and translate it into another. There are people who make a very good living from this sort of 'technology transfer'. Take a look at this."

Larry handed me a buff folder. He went off to fetch us some coffee while I skimmed through the case study.

Case study 1 – A copycat opportunity

Businesses often copy opportunities which were first spotted by their competitors. It is even possible to transfer ideas from one type of venture across to another – opportunity transfer. For example, a motor manufacturer could look at how a dairy farm operates; a theatre could study the way a hospital is run; a software consultancy could look over the fence (it wouldn't be a wall!) to a neighbouring timber merchant. In each case there might be obvious opportunities in the venture being studied that could be copied across or adapted in some way and then exploited.

But copycat opportunities are not limited to transfers between one business and another. Here's how a rapidly developing agrochemicals distributor used an aspect of the environment to study and re-engineer some of its key business processes.

They looked at the way a river begins its life in the hills and grows as it flows on its journey to the sea. In particular they considered the factors that influence the health of the river. Here are some of their observations and the questions they prompted:

- Streams that begin their life high up in the hills are more likely to grow into big rivers; those that start near the sea have limited scope for growth. (As a business, are we being realistic in our own growth expectations? What is a realistic growth rate given the position we are starting from?)
- High in the hills a stream grows rapidly as it takes in water from the steeply sloping land, but that is also where the stream is most likely to disappear altogether in prolonged dry weather. (During the early stages of our venture the growth potential may be greatest, but this is also when we will be most vulnerable to a cash-flow crisis.)
- If you take too much water out of a river you can cause serious environmental damage. This is most likely to be a problem during dry weather, and in drought years the river could dry up altogether, leaving those who rely on it for their water supplies in great difficulties. (Even when times are good we could damage our business if we take too much out rather than reinvesting, and we might not notice much of a problem until our markets go into recession.)
- Reservoirs in the upper reaches of a river can act as a buffer store, releasing extra water to maintain a healthy flow during the summer months. Not only can this create habitat diversity but it might also allow a wider range of water-based activities such as boating and water skiing. (Wise investment of some of our profits in the early years of the venture might enable us to diversify so that we are less vulnerable to downturns in one of our market sectors.)
- Long before a river stops flowing and dries up, most of its life – the aquatic insects, fish, water birds, and so on – has already been lost. Monitoring the health of plants and animals that depend on the river can give an early warning that something is amiss. Some species are extremely sensitive to pollution and their numbers can act as an indicator of water quality. (Long before we meet a cash-flow crisis and face collapse, there must be evidence that our business is heading for trouble. What should we be measuring? Which are the most sensitive indicators for our type of business?)

Most people would agree that there are advantages to be gained by keeping in touch with trends in your own market sector, but this was an interesting demonstration of the copycat technique used in a much less obvious way. It left me wondering how I could do something similar.

"The clever bit, I suppose," I said, "is to look across other industries and other service sectors, across different professions and so on, and not allow yourself to become too blinkered. I'll certainly be giving some thought to that."

Larry was grinning at me.

"What is it now?" I asked.

"I was just thinking. We really have got to shift your mind *away* from copying – at least to get you thinking in different ways and not just taking literally everything you hear."

"That's not fair!" I retorted. "If I disagree you say I'm unreceptive to new ideas, and if I agree you accuse me of following slavishly. I can't win with you, Larry."

"I want you to be a winner *without* me. That's my job. Not to create dependence but to encourage independent thought."

"OK – so what would you like me to say?" I asked, feeling that I was being treated like a child.

"Well, why don't you take the copycat concept and use it in some novel way? Technology transfer, as you call it, was a brilliant idea the first time it occurred to someone. Now there are whole armies of consultants feeding off companies like ours. They bring in ideas for change from other organisations. And they're not always relevant, good ideas, either."

I could see that there wasn't much chance of my finding better ways of doing my work by considering how other companies in other markets did things: I had spent all of my career to date in one industry, serving very narrow market sectors. Then I had a thought.

"I used to organise fund-raising for an environmental charity. I became very good at it, although I say so myself. Maybe I could make use of some of that experience. It was certainly quite different from anything we do here in Amsys."

"Good," Larry said. "Anything else?"

"Well, we used to have very good holidays. I guess I must have learned something from organising them."

"Anything else you *used to do*?" he prompted, emphasising the past tense.

I fell silent, feeling miserable. And I had just put into my own words what Mary had been trying to tell me for months – ever since the twins started school. My conversation now consisted of work and, in desperation, sometimes, reminiscences on things I *used to do*.

"Hadn't you better open up a few new opportunities to replace the ones you've closed down?" Larry asked.

I wanted to hit him, but I felt too weak.

"Cheer up," he continued. "It's not too late. Why not give some thought to making one of your 'used-to-do' experiences useful in your present job? And while you're at it how about creating a few outside-of-work opportunities for yourself and your family?"

I said I'd think about it. Larry just sat there, staring at me.

"I will. As soon as I get the time."

Too late; I had said it.

"All right," I told him, "I really will. At least one new idea from my used-to-do activities to help me here at work, and something new for outside work. By the end of the month. Ask me in three weeks' time. You see if I don't."

"No," Larry said. "I'm not going to ask. It's your life, Jim. You manage it."

I made myself a promise then, and I knew that if things were to improve I would have to keep it. Not for Larry's sake, nor just for my own, but also for Mary and the boys.

We sat in silence for a while: Larry seemed to understand what I was going through, though how he could have known I've no idea. He had no family commitments, and by all accounts he was coping very well with everything life threw at him. He never went out of his way to become popular, and yet somehow I felt he really did care – and not just for the company's sake, but for me as a person. Although his didactic, almost arrogant style was something I would not want to copy,

I found myself very much attracted to the ideas he was trying to put across. I would certainly be giving a lot more thought to finding copycat opportunities.

"OK," I said. "Let's leave that for now and talk about the second group, the windfalls, as you call them. It sounds to me as though these kinds of opportunities are nothing more than 'good luck'. Is that how you see it?"

"You're right, in a way," Larry replied. "All you have to do is to recognise an opportunity when you see one and then exploit it. This is still largely reactive management, and so I guess you *could* call it luck. Mind you, some people do seem to be much luckier than others. Ever wondered why?"

"I've thought about it," I told him, "but I can't say that I've come to any conclusion."

Larry smiled. "I have," he said. "Some of it must be due to mere chance, and as far as I know you can't do anything about that. But there are also plenty of opportunities that just turn up, out of the blue, and to spot them you have to be in the right place at the right time."

"Like finding wild mushrooms when you are out walking in the park?"

Larry nodded. "That's the general idea. Of course, it helps a lot if you spend time in the sorts of places where opportunities – mushrooms in this case – tend to occur more frequently. Try the meadows. Desert mushrooms aren't so common. Timing is usually important, too. For mushrooms, mid-winter is not a productive time."

It helps if you spend time where opportunities occur frequently

I could see Larry's point. "Are you saying that there is some way of working out where to be, and when to be there, so that you have more of these kinds of opportunities?" I asked.

"You're dead right there is! Have you ever heard anyone say, 'One day my ship will come in'?"

"Yes," I said. "Usually when they feel they've been unlucky and are hoping that one day they will get a lucky break. But in my experience they're only *saying* it – they don't really expect things to improve."

"That's right. Maybe their ship will come in one day. The problem is, as the saying goes, all too often they are waiting for it at an airport. Rather futile. To be consistently lucky, much luckier than average, you have to do something to deserve it."

To be consistently lucky, you have to do something to deserve good luck

"Even if it's just being in the right place – like joining the Navy if you want to see the world?" I asked.

"Er, possibly," Larry replied doubtfully. "But you know, Jim, these windfalls, as some people like to call them, are only worth having if you take advantage of them right away. Windfalls are usually quite conspicuous. If you don't act quickly, someone else is likely to spot them and pick them up. And in any case, they won't keep. Windfall opportunities need to be picked up right away, before they go off. So you see it's a two-stage process. First, spot the opportunity. Then take advantage of it right away, before someone else does."

"That sounds straightforward enough," I told him. "But how easy is it to recognise these sorts of opportunities?"

"If you know what sort of opportunity you want, you should be able to recognise it when it arises. Seek and you will find."

If you know what sort of opportunity you want, you should be able to recognise it when it arises

"Like mushroom gatherers recognising wild mushrooms?" I asked.

"Yes, that's the general idea," Larry replied. "Look. Here's another example. It shows how a farsighted entrepreneur was able to capitalise on a windfall opportunity."

Case study 2 – A windfall opportunity

This is an example of those kinds of opportunities that have to be seized without delay. If nobody spots the opportunity while it is fresh, it goes off, simply dissolving into non-existence.

Some years ago, British Telecommunications plc promoted its Yellow Pages directory of trade suppliers via a very successful television advertising campaign. In the advertisement, an elderly man (played by actor Norman Harknell) uses BT's Yellow Pages to search for a bookshop which still has a copy of an out-of-print book entitled 'Flyfishing, by J R Hartley.' At length the old man finds someone with a copy of the book and arranges to have it sent to him. The bookseller asks, "What name, sir?" and receives the reply: "Hartley – J R Hartley."

It was, of course, all make-believe. But with a strong script and brilliant acting the advert struck a chord with the general public.

And it might well have remained make-believe, but for one enterprising author/publisher team. Rather than put his own name on the cover, Michael Russell called his book 'Flyfishing, by J R Hartley'. It was, by all accounts, a good flyfishing book, benefiting from the expert advice of ace flyfisher Peter Lapsley; and in Britain a good flyfishing book sells typically a few thousand copies. This one did very much better: copies were bought as Christmas presents by the friends and families of just about everyone who was the slightest bit interested in fishing.

The timing was critical to success: the opportunity was greatest while the TV advertisement remained fresh in people's minds, and the timing of the book launch, just before Christmas, was also perfect.

Every year, a few dozen flyfishing books are published in Britain. Many other authors produced books that year, some of which must have been launched before Russell's. In principle, any one of those authors could have reassigned their writing to the fictitious J R Hartley; but Michael Russell did it, and as a result he and his enterprising publisher reaped a prolific windfall harvest.

Although I couldn't argue with Larry that Michael Russell had seen and exploited a very good windfall opportunity, it wasn't immediately obvious to me how I could apply the principle to my own work.

"Either you see such an opportunity or you don't," I told Larry. "And if no one had seen the J R Hartley opportunity, it would have gone begging. It would be too late in a few years' time."

"Right. So?" Larry prompted.

"Well, that's what I'm getting at. What can we do to make sure we don't waste those kinds of opportunities?"

Larry looked thoughtful. "It's pointless me saying 'Be in the right place at the right time', I'm sure. You'll just say 'How do you know when and where to be?' Perhaps another example will help. Imagine you work in Quality Assurance, and you intend visiting a potential supplier of components. Your aim is to vet that company in order to decide whether they are capable of supplying on time the quality and quantity you need. What would you look for?"

This was something I had actually done in the past, so I was on pretty safe ground. I said I would check every department involved in producing the components. I would assess whether they had the necessary resources: people, machinery, floor space and so on. And I would check their financial status, of course, to make sure they weren't about to go under.

"Ask to see their order book?" Larry asked.

I nodded. "Naturally," I said. "To make sure they really had enough future work. Er, but not too much."

"Good. So if you got satisfactory answers to all these points you would recommend that they be added to our Approved Suppliers list, and that would be another job done. Right?"

"Yes," I said, certain, now, that Larry held a rather different view.

"Don't worry," he said. "I'm not going to criticise. You obviously know more about supplier vetting than I do. But I think you would be missing an opportunity if that was *all* you did."

Larry went on to suggest that every visit to a customer, a

competitor, a collaborator or a supplier was an opportunity to improve market intelligence.

He was right. We were always complaining that our market information was incomplete and out of date, but most of us did nothing but complain about it.

"It makes sense," I told him. "But I've never heard of anybody writing up opportunity-management case studies before. How many have you collected so far?"

"Over the years? Several dozen. Anyway, if you're happy enough with that one shall we move on to the third group, the hidden opportunities? These are the ones you really have to hunt for. And of course, you also need to be able to recognise one when you've found it."

"OK. So now I guess we're operating much more in proactive mode," I said.

"That's right. You'll need to use your hunter-gatherer instinct to find these sorts of opportunities. Of course, it helps quite a bit if you have some idea what you are looking for – general characteristics rather than detailed descriptions. For example, you might decide that there are opportunities to get ahead of the opposition by teaming up with someone who has resources and skills that complement your own. Collaboration often works best if you avoid too rigid a definition of what contributions will be required of each collaborator. To me this suggests you should first find suitable partners and *then* agree to split responsibilities in whichever way maximises the benefits to all parties."

"All right. I follow that. But what other sorts of opportunities should I be looking for? In my work for Amsys, for instance?"

Larry gave me several examples, some of which amounted to simplifying products and processes so that people can under-stand them more easily and are less likely to make mistakes. He suggested that you can sometimes save people a lot of time and money by making things simpler – perhaps even so simple that the experts would mock and call it trivial. He quoted the single-station radio as an example of simplification carried to the extreme. You just plug it in and it works. No tuning knob, no volume control, nothing. Just a mains power plug with a radio and a loudspeaker built in. The radio comes pretuned for one of the most popular stations, and it costs so little that people are quite happy to buy two or three, one for each of their favourite stations.

It seemed such a brilliant idea, and yet I'd never seen it advertised. I asked him where I could get one.

Larry just grinned.

"You made that up!" I said.

"Sure. But it illustrates my point. Look around. You'll find lots of people doing very well by making things simpler. And maybe you'll see other opportunities of that type just waiting to be snapped up."

Larry and I talked a lot more about these kinds of opportunities. We agreed that cutting out unnecessary steps in procedures was another fertile area worth exploring. Larry said that a lot of what we do at work is a legacy of the past and is not necessarily relevant to today's needs. "And then there are always opportunities to reuse previous work," he added. "Reinventing the wheel must be costing business a fortune. And there are lots more kinds of opportunities, Jim. The trick is to find them before your competitors do."

"By looking ahead, you mean?"

Larry smiled. "That's the very best place to look if you want to find new opportunities!" he said.

Look ahead to find new opportunities

"That's not to say you can't learn from lost opportunities," he added.

Behind you there are only lost opportunities – Learn from them

He had a point. You don't need to be a genius to benefit from hindsight. But even twenty–twenty hindsight can only tell you what opportunities you have missed. Foresight is quite a different matter.

"Thinking ahead is the key to staying ahead," Larry continued. "Crisis managers rarely have time to think long term. An opportunity can come and go without them even recognising it, never mind making time to do anything about it. For these sorts of opportunities timing is often important. For example, I'm convinced that during economic recessions there are many more opportunities for those who go looking for them."

Thinking ahead is the key to staying ahead

"Hold on a minute, Larry!" I said. "Surely there is *less* opportunity, not more. There's *less* of everything in a recession, and that must make it a lot harder to find opportunities."

Myth
During economic recession, opportunities are a lot harder to find

"That's what you think! You and most other people," Larry replied. "But that's precisely the point. When times get hard, most people become extra cautious. They analyse things more thoroughly because the consequences of making a mistake *seem* to be greater. Even that may be more perception than reality. When money is tight, managers agonise over cash flow, credit control and the like. There are a lot more worried people out there, and so there are bound to be fewer creative people about."

"How do you make that out?" I demanded. I took my responsibility to manage the financial aspects of my job very seriously. Larry's suggestion was bordering on the offensive.

"Sore point, eh?" he asked. "Well, let me explain. When people are weighed down by worries they are unlikely to use their creativity to the full. Creativity is fun. It has to be, or it doesn't work. In a way you could say it is irresponsible, childish behaviour. Worried people generally try to behave in a more adult, more responsible way. By that I mean serious, cautious, logical, unadventurous. And *unimaginative*."

In a recession, more opportunity is available to the few people who can remain imaginative

"In a recession," Larry continued, "most business people become preoccupied with short-term results. They worry more than ever about risks and about the consequences of failure. If they are on the lookout for anything it is for risks rather than for opportunities. So, those people who spend at least part of their time looking for opportunities are likely to find more than their fair share."

People who spend time looking for opportunities are likely to find more than their fair share

"I see. So what you are saying is that there are fewer people hunting for opportunities, mainly because most people are concentrating on the risks that threaten their survival. But you can't really blame them. It's only human nature."

"It's the way most people *are*," Larry said. "And yet it needn't be so. Perhaps opportunity hunting is something of an acquired skill, but I'm convinced that it's also a basic part of our nature. A childish part that most adults try to suppress – if the education process hasn't already done so by the time they leave school."

I asked Larry whether there are any special techniques for opportunity hunting. He told me that it helps if you make a plan, setting out how and where you intend to search for opportunities and how you might exploit them when you find them. He said you need to be aware that some kinds of hidden opportunities have a habit of camouflaging themselves (they can even masquerade as risks), but the benefits are only available to those who see through the facade and recognise them and treat them as opportunities.

"What do you mean, *camouflage*?" I asked him.

"Well," he said. "Suppose you come across a lame old cart-horse in full harness. What would this conjure up in your mind?"

It was an odd sort of question, but I had a go at it: "Oh, I don't know – power, I suppose. And endurance – a bygone age. Is that the sort of thing you have in mind?"

"It's the future I have in mind," Larry said. "The poor old horse may not have much of a future. But keep hold of the harness."

And that, I thought, was an odd sort of answer.

"Sorry, Larry. I'm lost," I admitted.

"The point is this," Larry said earnestly. "Because the horse has no future most people would disregard the harness, too. But the harness has potential. Your challenge is to work out a future for the harness."

"I think I see what you're driving at. Are you saying that looking in a new way at familiar things, even those that might initially seem to be useless, can help us to discover hidden opportunities? Useful things whose potential isn't being exploited – is that the idea?"

"That's just one way of searching for opportunities," he said. "There are many others."

Larry suggested a process for finding opportunities in high-risk situations. You first describe the situation as you think (fear!) it might arise. Instead of putting all your effort into averting the risk, you can sometimes position yourself so that, whichever way things go, you benefit. (Heads you win, tails you win.) You ask yourself questions such as:

- What would have to be different for this to be a desirable situation?

There may be several answers; the trick is to find the easiest thing to change that will turn the situation from unsatisfactory to satisfactory.

Other useful questions are:

- For whom is this potentially good news?
- What would you have to do to become (or to team up with) the person or group for whom this is good news?

(Another way of expressing this is '*It's an ill wind that blows nobody any good.*')

What can you do to turn a risk into 'Heads you win; tails you win'?

- Can you make the situation more manageable by making it 'worse'? (Sometimes worse is better than bad!)
- If the present situation cannot be improved directly, can you create an opportunity by making it worse and then applying some of the other questions mentioned above?

Larry told me about a successful opportunity hunt he had heard of some years ago.

Case study 3 – Opportunity hidden within risk

This is an example of a successful search for opportunity within risk – in this case where the very survival of the company was at stake.

In the cut-throat world of film making, suppliers of support services are forever under pressure to deliver greater value for money. Those who build film sets rely for much of their profit margin on the salvage value of the materials they use. This is the story of a team which met a serious cash-flow crisis and used creative thinking to turn risk into opportunity.

Imagine the situation. You have built the set, the main street of a town, and filming is complete. Now you need to get a crew to dismantle the set so that you can salvage the timber and make some money – but you haven't got the cash to pay for the dismantling work. Now what do you do?

Would you:

- Borrow money, accepting that you would probably be charged such a high interest rate that there might be no profit in the job?

- Dismantle very slowly, or perhaps in phases, selling materials in smaller lots so that you could pay wages, and accept the increased transport costs that this would entail?

  or

- Cut your losses and go broke?

That's all it said. The rest of the page was blank.

"It's not all here," I said.

Larry waved the missing sheet and then hid it behind his back again.

"Well? What would *you* do?" he asked.

I considered the options listed. Jean would probably have opted for the first, because the outcome was pretty well guaranteed: lowest risk, but lowest return also. I rather favoured the second approach, pay as you go, although I recognised that it presupposed we could sell small lots when we needed to. This was more risky, and possibly no more profitable that the first option. I could see no merit in option three.

"I think I would choose number two," I told him.

Larry sighed. "You don't have to, you know," he said. "Just because I gave you a list doesn't mean you have to choose one of them. You could just do nothing and hope for a miracle."

Gifted manager I might not be, but I wasn't the wait-and-see type either. So what was Larry getting at?

"Are there other alternatives?" I asked.

"There might be. It's a risky situation, so there must be more than one solution. More than three, I'd say. For example, how many different ways can you think of for getting rid of the set and removing the materials from the site?"

I thought of taking it away intact, but that would be impossible. Maybe large chunks could be airlifted, but that would still leave me with the problem of dismantling it somewhere else. Perhaps some of the materials could be reused on site, although it would be an amazing coincidence if the next film just happened to need a very similar set to the one just completed. No, I could hardly count on that much good luck.

"I give up," I said. "How did they clear away the set and remain profitable?"

"They burnt it," Larry said.

"Gimmee!" I said, reaching for the missing page.

He was telling the truth.

Rather than dismantling the film set, they set fire to it. But before doing so they set up cameras at various angles and filmed the ensuing inferno with people running and screaming, silhouetted against the flames. The resulting footage was used in a number of films where a town fire was required. This proved to be a far more profitable venture as a result.

"The same idea has been applied to many similar situations, of course," Larry said. "In a whole range of films and TV programmes you will see the same train crashing over the side of a sabotaged bridge, a factory chimney toppling in a storm, or an office block collapsing after an explosion."

"OK, I'm convinced," I told him. "But so far everything you've talked about seems to apply to one-off jobs. Assignments and projects of one sort or another. Two-thirds of my work could be called 'business-as-usual'. Keeping things running. Supplying a service."

Then I told him about the problem I had had to deal with in Customer Support.

Larry smiled. "Sure, and isn't it easy to get into a rut? To keep on doing what you've always been doing. And that's fine if the rest of the world lets you get away with it. But all too often some sneaky competitor finds a better way, delivers a better service, and you start losing your customer base."

I shifted uneasily in my chair.

"Any suggestions?" I asked.

Larry told me how the manager of a hotel improved his return rate – the proportion of first-time clients who booked a subsequent stay at the hotel.

The problem was this: staff kept making mistakes and having accidents. A room would get missed from the servicing schedule; a steak would be cooked well done when the client had ordered a rare steak; a waiter would trip and pour wine all over the tablecloth or, worse still, over a client. And not every upset client would complain; the majority would say nothing at the time, but would then spend the next six months telling and retelling the disaster story to all their friends and acquaintances: *"I wouldn't go there if I were you – It's awful!"*

Staff training was obviously the key. But no matter how much money and time you pour into training people, they still make mistakes, and then you end up with perhaps ninety-nine satisfied customers mentioning your hotel to nobody, and one disgruntled customer going around telling dozens of people how awful you are.

Here's how this enterprising hotel manager turned the risk of an accident into an opportunity. His staff still receive training, but instead of trying to develop people to such a standard of professionalism that everything runs like clockwork – efficient reception and porterage, perfectly clean rooms, excellent cuisine and super-fast service – they concentrate a significant part of the training on managing complaints. Here's how it works . . .

For whatever reason, a waiter spills wine on the tablecloth. Maybe he is careless; maybe he catches his heel on a pulled thread in the carpet; maybe a customer suddenly pushes back from the table or waves to an acquaintance across the restaurant. The end result is the same: you get wine splashed down your shirt front.

Immediately you are ushered to a private room and given a clean shirt to change in to. Your party is moved to a fresh table, a new bottle of wine and a magnum of champagne are brought to your table at no charge, even though you were well into the original bottle of wine; and at the end of the meal your bill is waived. And suppose the person whose extravagant gesture was the cause of the accident is also very upset. No problem: she receives a complimentary bottle of wine, too.

And afterwards? Chances are you will return again and again. And for sure you will tell any number of people about the incident. *"The staff were brilliant,"* you say. *"No panic. No recriminations. They handled the situation without making a drama of it, and everyone had a superb evening."*

"And what has it cost the hotel to have an unpaid salesman?" Larry asked. "Because that's what you are doing: you are selling their professionalism to all your friends and acquaintances. A meal and couple of bottles of plonk? Pretty good value, eh?"

"I'd say so," I said.

"So you see," Larry concluded, "zero complaints is not only an unrealisable target, it's also not necessarily the best way to win people's loyalty and get them to become your ambassadors."

Zero complaints is neither an achievable target nor a desirable one

Larry suggested that planning how you will deal with problems and being prepared for them is often a better strategy than trying to avoid problems altogether.

I needed to apply this idea to our customer support work. Once the Bilston bid had gone out of the door I would get together with John Scriven and plan some training in complaints handling.

Planning how you will deal with problems and being prepared for them is usually better than trying to avoid them altogether

"OK," I said. "Perhaps we should leave the matter of hidden opportunities that you have to go hunting for, and talk about the fourth type."

"Right. These don't just turn up, and they're not tucked away somewhere waiting for you to stumble across them. These are the opportunities that only exist if you create them – the ultimate in proactive opportunity management."

"It sounds fantastic. Can anyone play?" I asked.

Larry ignored my sarcasm. "I'm sure most people *could*," he said, "but very few do. The key to opportunity creation is imagination, and not everyone knows how to find the 'on' switch for their imagination."

Imagination is the key to creating opportunities

I tried to imagine what it must be like to have no imagination. I couldn't, so I just nodded and Larry continued: "You have to picture a world that does not exist. Then in your imagination, you make the journey from your new world back to the one you are living in right now."

"Back to reality, you mean?" I asked.

"I wouldn't put it quite that way. Back from the future, maybe. One day the world in your imagination could be as real as the world you are living in now, once you exploit the opportunity you have created. On the journey back from your new world to the present you have to blaze a trail through or around many obstacles. In so doing you are creating the road between the then and the now. When you succeed, you have made your future world into the new now. Other people will be able to use your trail and travel the journey after you."

If I had said something as weird as that I would have been embarrassed. I would have mumbled an apology and slunk away in shame. But Larry didn't. He really was comfortable talking that way. The trouble was, he expected it to mean something to people like me. It didn't.

"Do you think you could come back down to earth now, Larry?" I said. "You've lost me completely. It's a good job Jean isn't listening in on this."

"OK. Perhaps an example will help. Suppose a lumberjack and a poet walk through the same forest. What do you suppose they see? Start with the lumberjack."

"Trees?" I offered.

"All right. And what else?" Larry pressed.

"How should I know? I've not been there. If it's not trees then I give up!"

"He sees trees, of course," Larry said. "But he probably also sees a whole load of problems. Work that has been done badly. Work that needs doing urgently. A whole lot of trimming and thinning. And no doubt even bigger problems stored up for the future, when the time comes to harvest the timber."

"I see. And the poet?" I asked, going for a pre-emptive strike.

"Only the poet could answer that. Maybe a face in the bark of an old oak. Imaginary fairy folk flitting to and fro among hollyhocks that don't really exist beside a sylvan stream that isn't really there either. A unicorn with a golden horn. If he's imaginative he could find anything he wanted."

"Yes, but it wouldn't be real," I retorted. Larry was ready for that one.

"Is the trimming and thinning work any more real to the poet than the unicorn to the lumberjack?" he asked. "What I would ask you is this: if someone goes through life looking for problems what do you think they find?"

"Problems," I replied instinctively.

Go through life always looking for problems and problems are all you will find

"That's right. And since there is no shortage of problems, the quest is invariably successful, justifying the decision to spend time looking for problems. And this is fine if it results in wiser decisions and better plans. But in the same way, if that same someone were to look for opportunities, expecting to find them, then the chances are they would find opportunities."

"Oh, I get it," I said. "If you believe that it is possible to see a unicorn then you will be able to see one, even though you have to create it in your mind's eye. And the same with creating opportunities. It's only possible if you believe that it is possible. Is that what you're suggesting?"

To create an opportunity you must first believe in the possibility

"Yes, I am," Larry agreed.

"But it's still only imaginary," I said doubtfully.

Larry beamed. "That's right," he said. "An opportunity doesn't become reality just because someone sees it, but it will never become reality if no one sees it."

An opportunity will never become reality unless someone sees it

"OK. I get the general idea," I told him. "But I would have a hell of a job convincing Jean on this one. It might help if you could give me a simple, practical example. But please – not fairies, no sylvan streams of subconsciousness or whatever. Let's have something from the harsh world of reality. The world of nuts and bolts and delivery deadlines and paying the mortgage."

Larry stared at me – through me – for a few moments. "All right," he said. "Let's try it. Can you imagine this happening? You win a contract to do some work for a customer at an agreed price. Then, you get the customer to do a large part of the work. When the job is finished the customer pays the agreed price plus an extra payment for being allowed to do the work himself. *And* – and this is very important – your customer is totally delighted and keen to do more business with you in the future."

"Grow up!" I retorted. "You're talking complete nonsense."

"No, Jim. Whatever you do, don't grow up," Larry insisted. "I asked if you could *imagine* it happening."

"Of course not. The customer would have to be a blithering idiot. Bilstons aren't fools, and neither are any of the other people we do business with."

"Picture the unicorn," Larry urged.

I closed my eyes and tried. "It's no good, Larry, I can't picture anything. I'm tired," I said.

"You work too hard. That's why you're always tired. And that's why you find it hard to be imaginative. But if you *could* satisfy your customers in this way, just think of the advantages. There would be a lot less pressure on you and your team, for a start. You might even have time to do some of the important things really well. Imagine it!"

Work too hard for too long and you get over-tired; then you become less imaginative

I could still recall those far-off days when life seemed carefree and so much more fun. But there was no going back – I realised that. And yet I couldn't help thinking that things would be better if only I could have a bit more time. Time just to myself. Time to think things through properly without the incessant pressure of performance targets and deadlines. I was sure it would make a world of difference.

"You're right, Larry," I agreed. "It *would* be great, if only it were possible. For a start we could agree a more flexible delivery schedule. And I would get a lot less hassle from Jean over budgets. And another thing . . ."

"Right! *Now* close your eyes. Can you see the unicorn?" Larry asked.

I wanted to. I closed my eyes and gave it a try.

It worked.

"Yes, I can," I said in amazement. "It's silver and blue with a great big golden horn, and it's perched on a flat rock on the top of a grassy hill."

Larry grinned. "I think we've found a future for that harness," he said. "Don't lose the unicorn. It can take you anywhere you want to go."

"It can?"

"Definitely! But first you need to harness your unicorn," he said.

To secure unique opportunities, you need to harness the unicorn

"Eh?"

"All you need to do is to set up and manage a plan for making it happen," Larry persisted. "And then make it happen."

"Right," I said. "An opportunity-creation plan. But I've still got the problem of convincing Jean. You wouldn't happen to have another of those real-life case studies, would you? It might help me a lot if I could show Jean how someone else had harnessed the unicorn of opportunity."

"Sure," Larry said, and then he explained how an imaginative entrepreneur made something from nothing by using creative thinking processes and proactive opportunity management.

Case study 4 – An imagineered opportunity

This is an example of the power of unconventional thinking and of challenging the assumptions that limit the effectiveness of traditional approaches to problem solving.

Can you describe a wheelbarrow? Of course you can: one wheelbarrow is pretty much the same as another. They vary in size and in colour, maybe. But that's about all. And there's a very good reason for this conformity: there's not a lot of scope for creativity. Wheelbarrows are commodity items. Every wheelbarrow consists of a container (the barrow) shaped so that it's easy to shovel stuff in and easy to tip it back out when you want to, a pair of handles, and a wheel so you can push the thing along.

Let's challenge those assumptions – that's exactly what a man called James Dyson did.

Do we really need the container? Of course. Without that the wheelbarrow would be useless as a means of shifting stuff from place to place. And it needs to be the right sort of shape for shovelling stuff into and for tipping stuff out again. OK, so we'll need a container much the same as the barrow on anyone else's wheelbarrow.

And the handles? Sure, unless we're in the totally different market of powered machinery we will need a means of grabbing hold of the thing to shift it from one place to another. And over the centuries barrow-handle design has been fine-tuned pretty much as far as it can go. Let's stick with conventional handles, then.

And finally the wheel. We'll need a wheel, of course, or we won't be able to shift the thing from one place to another. But hang on a moment – what we really need is a means of shifting the barrow. A wheel is one possibility, but let's not allow our thinking to get into a rut (as wheelbarrows frequently do on soft ground).

James Dyson didn't fit a wheel to his barrow. He used a ball.

The Dyson Ballbarrow does everything that a wheelbarrow can do, and it has the added advantage that it is less prone to creating ruts in soft ground. It can go where traditional wheelbarrows simply cannot.

Within three years, the Ballbarrow became the market leader. And all because Dyson's imaginative mind was prepared to ignore conventional wisdom, challenge assumptions and so create a new concept.

Dyson is no one-product wonder. He has applied imagineering to a whole range of products from amphibious vehicles to vacuum cleaners, and has built up a world-class multinational business as a result.

"So really," I said, "it's all about being different."

Larry agreed. He said that there were numerous examples of successes built on one unique factor. He quoted an example from a declining service, the doorstep delivery of milk.

Until quite recently, there was a very successful business – a two-man family firm – delivering milk and dairy products to the homes of people in a Hampshire village. They didn't deliver milk as early as some of their competitors could, but they retained the loyalty of their clients at a time when more and more people were switching to cut-price milk collected from the supermarket.

Their uniqueness? They delivered everything by bicycle. The older man would call with the milk and ask his customer if they needed cream, eggs or butter.

"I'll send the nipper round with it," he would say, as he had been saying for quite some time. The nipper (his son) was seventy, and the older man well into his nineties when, through failing health, the old man eventually hung up his cycle clips.

We talked about some of the other opportunities born out of questioning traditional approaches. On a global scale the Sony Walkman was an example of challenging the assumption that hi-fidelity sound belonged in a big box in the home. One assumption brushed aside; a unique selling point discovered; an opportunity created.

Why hadn't I looked at things this way before? Probably for the same reason most people didn't: because they were too busy worrying about problems (and the risks involved in changes that might bring yet more problems) to think about opportunities.

So if Larry was right there were at least four distinct types of opportunity.

Types of opportunity:

- Copycat opportunities
- Windfalls
- Hidden opportunities, masquerading as risks
- Imagineering

There just had to be opportunities, like those in the case studies, waiting for me and my team. If only we could find them. If only we could discover how to make them come true. Maybe I could learn about that from Larry.

"Thanks for all that," I said. "It's pretty convincing. I think at last the basic concepts are becoming clearer. One thing's for sure, Larry: I'm definitely going to have to change my approach to work. I must have been missing opportunities all my life without ever being aware of it. Still, at least I now realise just how little I do know about opportunity management. Stage two. Conscious incompetence."

"We're all learning," Larry replied with a grin. "What's the reading on your funometer right now?"

"Eh?"

"Are you enjoying yourself?" he asked.

I had to admit that I was enjoying it, even if the learning process was a bit on the slow side. I understood Larry's four categories of opportunity. And, even though I felt sure the case studies wouldn't cut much ice with Jean Cartwright, they had convinced me of one thing: opportunity management really can work. Now what I needed, and quickly, was to create risk and opportunity management plans for the Bilston job. I asked Larry if he would give me a hand.

"There's no time like the present, Jim," he replied. "Almost every opportunity has a limited shelf life. Why don't you get started and I'll join you in a day or two. You can always call me if you get really stuck."

Most opportunities have a limited shelf life

"OK," I agreed. "But I really need your help right now, to get started. I think I understand the different types of opportunities and what to do to benefit from each type. The trouble is, I haven't a clue how to go about planning that sort of thing. And I'm quite sure Jean doesn't believe in unicorns, so there's no point in asking her."

Larry laughed. "All right," he said. "But before we go into the details of opportunity management it would be worth looking at some of the things you can do to identify and manage risk. Then you will see how they link in with the sorts of things that can help you to manage opportunity."

Larry stood up and moved towards the door. He stopped and turned to me.

"You know, Jim, some day soon you should come across to my department and look at one or two of our plans. You would see how we use proactive *and* reactive risk-management techniques. Then, as I said, once you're happy with the risk side of things, we can move on to looking at ways of managing opportunity, too. It's much easier to create an opportunity-management plan once you have a reasonably good idea of the risks in a job, as I'll show you when you get to that stage. OK?"

"You bet!" I told him. "That would be great. Thanks, Larry – Oh, good grief! Is that the time? I ought to be preparing for this evening's meeting."

"Right, I'll leave you in peace. But we could make a start on your risk-management plan over lunch tomorrow. If Jean says you can spare the time, that is."

"I'll decide my own priorities," I told him. "See you tomorrow lunch-time. And – thanks, Larry. It's been useful. Sorry I've got to cut this short."

Larry departed, whistling contentedly. He never seemed to be under pressure. Lucky devil!

Half an hour and three interruptions later I was still thinking all these things over when Mary phoned to remind me that the twins were in a concert after school that evening.

"Of course I hadn't forgotten," I said. "Not quite. I'm on my way . . . No, a snack after the concert will do me fine. I've hardly had time to digest lunch."

(The last bit, at least, was true.)

I gathered up a pile of paperwork, stuffed my briefcase until the hinges creaked under the pressure, and set off before the phone could get me again.

Jill, Pete and Nadia were working late in the bid room. They would just have to run their review meeting without me for once.

I slunk past them feeling guilty – and feeling confused, annoyed and even more guilty that I should feel *any* guilt for wanting to see my boys in their very first concert.

One thing was clear: if I was going to crack this time-management thing and start enjoying life again, it wasn't going to be by working longer hours. Larry was right. I had got to learn how to manage opportunities.

It was very late that evening before I had a chance to update my opportunity-management notebook.

Opportunity: identifying features, habitat and behaviour

- Copying other people's opportunity-management initiatives won't make you a winner, but it can help you to keep up with the pack.
- Some opportunities are just waiting to be recognised and exploited; others need proactive management.
- Chance may be random, but it is certainly possible to become luckier – not by merely wishing, but by doing something to earn it.
- Planning to be in the right place at the right time is a good way to become luckier.
- Hunt for hidden opportunities, but remember that they often masquerade as risks.
- Look ahead for new opportunities; behind you there are only lost opportunities.
- Thinking ahead is the key to staying ahead.
- In difficult times many people become obsessed with risks; this leaves more opportunities for the few who remain imaginative.
- Like harnessing the unicorn, creating opportunities is only possible if you believe that it is possible.
- Imagination is the key to opportunity creation.
- Go through life always looking for problems, and problems are all you will find.
- To create an opportunity you must first believe in the possibility.
- An opportunity will never become reality if no one sees it.
- Most opportunities have a limited shelf life.

Action: I must review my plans to see whether I can turn some of the risks into opportunities.

Chapter 4

Risk: the nature of the beast

I made sure that Jean got to see Larry's case studies in opportunity management. If *I* couldn't convince her the idea had merit, maybe *they* would. If not, then nothing would.

They didn't.

"There's nothing earth-shattering here, Jim," Jean said when I dropped in to her office to pick up a late revision of the Bilston tender documents. "I wish you wouldn't keep wasting your time on this junk. You're getting carried away by a lot of fancy words that boil down to nothing more than hindsight and post-rationalisation. I could write up any number of case studies for successful jobs I've been involved in over the years. And a few horror stories. When you look back on a venture it's always possible to ascribe success to some lucky break that appeared to make all the difference in the world. You might just as well blame every failure on the vagaries of chaos theory – that's not to say some of the worst disasters aren't made that much worse by bad luck. By and large, though, I reckon it's self-delusion to claim that some brilliant initiative you took caused it all to happen the way it did. On the whole, you succeed because you deserve to succeed, and you deserve to succeed if you are more committed and more thorough than your competitors – in other words you work harder than they do. Unless of course you're incompetent or careless, in which case you deserve to be unlucky and you ought to fail every time."

"Do you *really* believe that?" I asked. "These case studies – do you think Larry just made them up? These are real companies. Companies like ours. Only they're not quite like us, because they are successful. And they're successful because they manage risks professionally and because they manage opportunities just as professionally. In other words they work smarter, not necessarily harder."

"Calm down, Jim. I'm all in favour of a professional approach to everything we do, and that includes risk management. And I'm more than happy for you to get help from Farlow or anyone else who can help us make a better job of this bid. But can't you see that all these fancy words and slogans about managing opportunity don't alter a thing? I've been through all this idealism and dreaming nonsense. What you never see in case studies like these are all the dreams that never came true. There's no substitute for logical reasoning based on fact. Fact, not fantasy. Real opportunity management simply means running your business more efficiently than your competitors. And that can be boiled down to plain old-fashioned common sense and hard work. These have always been the ingredients of success, and they always will be." She could see I was shaking my head and waiting to get in with an objection, but she pressed on with her cathartic tirade. "I've been around a lot longer than you have, Jim, and I know that some things do *not* change. I've always believed in the principle that there's no such thing as a free lunch or a free anything else. You don't get owt for nowt, and I've no intention of pinning my hopes on a 'something for nothing' philosophy."

"But Jean – have you actually *read* any of the case studies? None of them is about efficiency. They're all to do with becoming more *effective*. Tell me honestly, *did* you read them?"

For a moment Jean looked uneasy. "I've read quite enough, thank you. Enough to know that the so-called principles don't stand up to critical analysis. There's no logic to it. These are just a heap of random, unconnected events. There's no cause and effect. No rational process. In a nutshell, it's just not business-like. Business works by logic, not magic."

Pleased with her neat turn of phrase, Jean thrust the case studies at me with a dismissive flourish. As far as she was concerned, that was the end of the matter.

"I'll need a one-to-one with you to go through that risk-management plan as soon as it's ready," she said. "How's it coming along?"

"Well – OK, I suppose. It'll be a while before we've got everything together, but I can show you what we've done so far if you like."

Jean shook her head emphatically. "No thanks. I've had quite enough glimpses of the incomplete and the unsupportable. I need to see the whole picture if I'm to support your plans when they come up for the chief exec's approval. We need something that is capable of standing close scrutiny if it's going to convince Bilstons. Call Sandra when you've got your act together. She'll arrange a slot in my diary for us to review the plan. We'll need a couple of hours when everyone is fresh. There will be loads of data to analyse. An early morning start would be best."

Loads of data? Not in my plan there wasn't! It might withstand a cursory glance, but the idea of close scrutiny was unnerving.

On the surface the basic plan appeared convincing, but the risk assessment was all very broad-brush and I knew that Jean would not be amused. She expected every loose end to be tied down. Still, this was the first time we had made any sort of risk-management plan at the bidding stage. It was a big step forward for us, and what there was had been quantified, so at least we would have *some* figures to review. With a bit of luck that might keep the dragon off my back so that I could concentrate on editing the proposal.

But I still felt uneasy. Would the plan satisfy Bilstons? There was nothing in their request to tender saying how much detail they expected to see in a risk-management plan, and I had no idea what form they would expect it to take. There was one reassuring thought, though: we knew a lot more about this type of work than Bilstons did. They wouldn't be coming to us if they could do the job themselves. If Bilstons wanted us to do the work, they would have to trust our judgement. After all, it was a fixed-price contract. We were the ones taking the financial risk, not they.

But what if Bilstons didn't want to take our plans on trust? If we couldn't convince them that we knew how to manage the job, with whatever risks that entailed, they might decide to give the contract to someone else. There were bound to be plenty of bidders – nobody in our industry was so flush with work that they could afford to put in anything short of their very best offer.

There was no alternative: I had to get a second opinion on our risk-management plan, while there was still time to change it if necessary. One option was to make a fuss, to insist on Jean looking through the rough draft. She would try to wriggle out of it, complain that it was a waste of her valuable time, and give me a lot of Arctic body language to make me feel an incompetent wimp. But I had a perfect right to ask for her help. It wasn't so much admitting inadequacy as taking the teamwork approach. After all, two heads are better than one. To hell with my personal pride. I could *insist* on getting her help. If necessary I could grovel and plead with her to give me a hand. She would have no choice.

I asked Larry, instead.

The Bilston contract was an interesting one. Bilstons had invited us to put in a fixed-price bid for updating the South Morestead to Delvington communications link. It was part of a major investment programme that included a new jetty and warehouse complex at Delvington Port, an elevated trunk route to take traffic from the harbour round rather than through the town, and a new communications and control centre at South Morestead, near the airport. Bilstons were prime contractors for the whole of the work – we weren't quite in that league. They were doing most of the civil engineering work themselves, but calling in specialists for the computer systems, the control gear and most of the communications facilities. Like the main contract itself, all subcontracts were being let on a fixed-price basis with small incentives for early completion and much higher penalties for lateness. And you couldn't blame Bilstons for this: it was a buyer's market and they had plenty of bidders keen to win orders almost at any price. We knew it was going to be a tough competition. It wasn't quite our normal line of work, but it would help to fill a gap in our workload until new contracts came through from our regular customers. We had more than a dozen big tenders outstanding around the world, but the market was slow and most of our customers were delaying or scaling down their investment programmes.

On the face of it, the job we were bidding for seemed pretty straightforward: replace the communications equipment at each end of the link, refurbish the local area networks throughout the buildings, add some new security facilities. But there were some scary risks, not the least of which was the cooling system for the Delvington transmitter. It can get pretty hot and humid out there.

With Pete's help, Jill, Nadia and Dave had worked out an estimate for the cost of each chunk of work – the equipment, the civil engineering works, installation testing and training. They had added on our management and on-site administration charges and that gave a figure for the basic cost estimate.

The next bit is always tricky: the risk assessment. They had rated each part of the job according to its inherent risk – high, medium or low. On this job most of the risks were at least medium and several had been rated as high. Then the risk planning involved building in contingencies: 50 per cent for high risks, 5 per cent for medium and 1 per cent for low.

Following their evening review meeting, the team members were reasonably happy with the risk-management plan. It looked good to me, too. I showed it to Larry, together with some of the estimates.

"Is this *it*?" he asked. "You call this a risk-management plan?"

"Yes. Well – no. I mean, there's still a lot more to be done," I assured him. "The next step is pricing the bid. There are other expenses and overheads that have to be added in to give the overall cost of the work. And on top of all this we put a profit mark-up to get a first stab at the selling price. What happens then is . . ."

Larry was looking increasingly uncomfortable. He made an uncharacteristic interruption: "That's scrambled logic, if you want my opinion."

"Wait a minute, Larry," I said. "I hadn't finished. What happens then is that our sales and marketing people compare this figure with what they think the customer is expecting to pay. And of course, they also have to take a guess at our major competitors' prices for the job. Invariably this means that I have to reduce all the estimates, sometimes by as much as 30 per cent. But the important thing is, I always try to keep *something* in reserve for contingencies. It's a system that we have developed over many years. What do you think?"

"I'm amazed," Larry said.

"Impressed?" I asked, none too hopefully.

"No, just amazed," he replied with a sigh. "Amazed that you win any contracts at all. And I'm not in the least bit surprised that you overspend your budgets and that most of your work is way behind schedule. This isn't a risk-management plan. This isn't any kind of plan."

"Hold on, Larry," I told him. "We do make a work schedule, too – a great big chart showing what follows what, and which activities can go on in parallel. We even use a computer to tell us how long the whole job will take."

"Do you mean how long it will take *if* all goes to plan?" Larry asked.

"Well yes, naturally," I agreed.

"Which it never does – you have already *admitted* that."

I felt trapped. Larry was quite right, of course.

"That's what worries me most of all," I said. "It's why I hate these high-risk jobs. If only customers would ask us for things that we know all about!"

"We've been through all that," Larry replied. "You can't expect to make a living by reliving the past. If you want my opinion, Jim, this so-called risk-management plan is going to bring you a lot of grief. And I very much doubt whether it's going to help you at all in managing the risks."

"It *will*!" I retorted. "It gives me the money I'll need to pay for the extra work that will be necessary when things go wrong. Without it I wouldn't be able to stick to the plan."

Larry slumped back in his chair and stared incredulously at the wall behind my head. Then he got up and walked over to the window. With his back to me he said, coolly: "When things go wrong, sticking to the plan is almost invariably the wrong thing to do. You are aware of that, aren't you?"

Myth
A manager's job is to make a
plan and then to ensure that it is
followed

In the short time I had know him, I had never known Larry to joke about anything. A strange feeling of unease came over me – something in between doubting the existence of the Tooth Fairy and fearing that Gravity might at any moment take a holiday.

"You're having me on, aren't you?" I replied. "How can I possibly get the job finished if I don't stick to the plan? And in any case, there's no point in making a plan if you don't intend to use it."

Larry's eyebrows rose and he stared through me for what felt like half a lifetime. "Who said anything about not *using* the plan? Your job is to ensure that the goals are met – delivering the goods and services on schedule and within budget, and at the end of the contract having a customer who is delighted with your performance and wants to do business with you again."

"Well, yes. But I thought that was what the plan was for."

A manager's job is to keep changing the detail of the plan in order to achieve the goals

"There's a very big difference between sticking to a plan and *using* a plan," Larry said.

"Is there really?" I asked sheepishly. "Then perhaps you had better tell me about it."

"All right. But first of all you need a plan that is worth using, and that means making the risks an integral part of the plan – not bolting them on afterwards as you seem to have been trying to. Planning ahead is useful because it makes you *think* ahead – in particular, to think about the risks and the opportunities that might lie ahead."

The main benefit of planning ahead is that it makes you think ahead

Opportunities. That word again. I needed to learn more, especially about opportunities and how to manage them.

Larry sat back for a while and studied the figures in our plan. I could see another inquisition brewing.

"For a start, what do the 50, 5 and 1 per cent figures mean?" he asked. "The chance that you won't be able to do it at all? How much more it might cost? How much longer the work might take? Or what?"

Obviously I had failed to get across to Larry just how urgent this job was. He still seemed to think that taking longer was an option.

"You don't seem to understand," I told him. "It's no use us asking Bilstons for more time. There isn't any. If we can't do the job when Bilstons want it then we won't get the contract. We can't have any more time, we've got to make it work, and it's a fixed-price contract so there won't be any more money."

"OK, so what *do* the figures refer to?" Larry asked, pointing to the 'Risk' column.

"It's the level of *risk*," I said. Larry still looked unhappy, so I went through the process in more detail.

"It's like this," I told him. "We discuss and decide how risky each task is. Then, for the high-risk ones, we allocate 50 per cent extra in the draft budget – that's to allow for dealing with any problems. The medium risks get an extra 5 per cent and the low risks get just 1 per cent."

"Oh, really?" Larry said. "So let's see if I've got this. A high-risk task is one where you believe you will need 50 per cent more money than you estimate would be needed to do the work if it contained no risks at all. Is that right?" Larry asked.

"Well, yes, I suppose so," I replied cautiously.

"Frankly, Jim, I think that's monstrous. You don't appear to have spent much time thinking about the risks, at all . . ."

"That's not true!" I snapped. "Five of us spent all last Friday going right through the Bilston estimates to decide where the risks were."

"And *what* they were?" he asked.

I didn't see what he was getting at, and I told him so.

That was the first time I ever saw Larry looking confused. Something was obviously bothering him, and I had a nasty feeling it ought to be bothering me, too.

"Quite honestly, I think we ought to put away your plan – for now, at least," he suggested. "Let's just talk about risk."

Larry did most of the talking. He told me that risks come in various guises, each type requiring a different management approach. He said that some risks were associated with general uncertainty – for example uncertainty about the cost or the duration of an activity, or with unpredictability of the queuing time before work gets underway. These uncertainties are due to random factors such as the weather, or traffic hold-ups, or simply the day-to-day variable enthusiasm of the people doing the work. So when all goes well a particular task might take, say, four hours; the norm could be nearer five; but on a really bad day it might take ten hours or more to get the job done.

**When things go exceptionally
well you save time, but nothing
like the amount you can lose if
things go badly**

That certainly fitted in with my own experience.

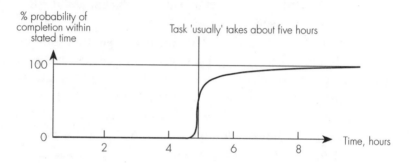

As Larry explained it, this type of uncertainty affects just about every activity. The uncertainty tends to diminish with time (just as opportunities do), so that the nearer you get to completing a job the more confident you become of the final cost and the actual completion date. In the course of time all the risks resolve into certainties. But as you get nearer to completion so there are fewer opportunities for taking initiatives that can influence the value of the job.

**Risks resolve –
as opportunities dissolve**

By way of example he cited the problem of predicting how much you would have to pay for imported materials that are to be delivered at some future date, given the situation where financial exchange rates fluctuate from day to day. The difference between today's exchange rate and tomorrow's is unlikely to be much, but over a twelve-month period the rate could easily change by a great deal.

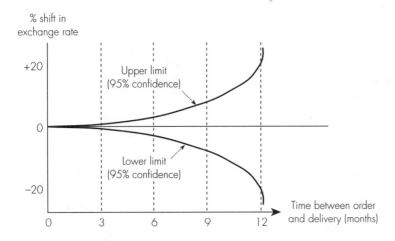

Larry said that when building up an estimate for a task you should start with the bits you understand – the well-defined work. This means all of the work where, if required, you could say exactly what needs to be done, how you intend doing it, what materials you will need, and so on. You understand this part of the job well, because it is very similar to work you have done many times before. Based on past experience you can estimate fairly accurately how long this would take and how much it would cost, taking into account the number of people in the team, their skills and experience, what tools and other resources they will be able to use, and so on. A whole load of such factors influence the result, but you should be able to come up with a figure on the assumption that the necessary work gets done right first time.

In addition, there are always other things that you have to do, although you cannot say in advance exactly what they will be. What you can be sure of is that they will be very real when you come to do the job. This part of the work is ill defined because you don't have a very clear view of the future – not on those parts of the job that are unlike anything you've done before – and because the goals are never crystal clear despite all your efforts to specify the scope of the work. In this category you can also include the time spent chasing essential information, keeping other people informed, asking for help, and being interrupted by other people asking *you* for help. This uncertain element of the work is difficult to estimate, which means there is a range of actual durations and costs. So, you have to make a judgement – that's what estimates really are.

Then, Larry told me, if you are sensible you add on an allowance for scrap – work that has to be done again because of various little mistakes. Most jobs take somewhat longer and cost a little more than they need because people keep on making the same mistakes. (We don't like the word 'mistakes'; we prefer the euphemism 'rework'.) Estimating for rework is a matter of experience, and the amount depends on the nature of the job and on the people doing it.

"I can see some merit in breaking the estimate down in this way," I said. "It does make you ask yourself how well you understand the work you are estimating for."

"That's right," Larry agreed. "It also forces you to face up to the issues of scrap and rework and, in particular, to set targets for reducing them and getting more things right first time. Shall we move on?"

I nodded, and Larry drew a sketch showing the components of an estimate.

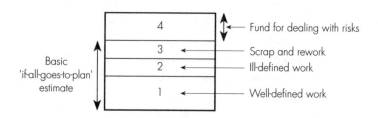

"Next you need to consider the risks," Larry continued. "These are the potential causes of serious setbacks that can cause you to change your whole approach. At the very least they present you with crises to sort out. Any part of a job containing significant risks needs very careful handling. Later, if you like, I'll show you how you can make a plan for managing risk and opportunity. For now, though, you need to decide how you would cope with such eventualities. Then, estimate the extra time, cost and resources you would need. You can think of this as the implications of doing nothing to limit the risk and either living with or dealing reactively with its consequences."

I asked Larry to tell me more about major risks.

He said they can be quite different from minor uncertainties such as how efficient a worker might be or how many faulty items there might be in a batch of purchased supplies. Major risks can be thought of as a chance selection between two or more possible futures. As an example he cited a parachute opening or not opening. A paratrooper cannot be absolutely sure in advance which of these alternative outcomes will apply, but his future would be very different in each case – in the one case perhaps spanning many years; in the other most likely just a matter of seconds.

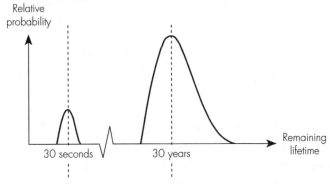

Larry sketched what he called a life-expectation curve. He asked me what the paratrooper could do to reduce the probability associated with the first peak in the curve. I suggested he could check that his parachute was properly attached, and maybe even have a second parachute in case the first one didn't open. Larry agreed and said it was also advisable to stay on friendly terms with whoever packs the parachutes. Better still, *be* the one who stays on the ground packing parachutes.

"Right. I follow all that. So in general are you saying the estimate gets bigger because of all the extra things you do to manage risk?" I asked.

Larry shook his head. "Not really. It becomes more realistic. What I mean is that the estimate may well get bigger, but on the other hand you are also a crucial step nearer to having a proactive plan for managing risk and opportunity. You now know exactly which areas to concentrate on."

I just had to ask the question.

"What do you mean, *proactive* risk management?"

Larry had been expecting it. "These are things you intend doing over and above the basic minimum," he said. "For example, measures you might take so that risks, if they materialise, will have less impact and will be more manageable, and so that you can find and capitalise on some of the opportunities inherent in those risks."

"OK. I think I follow that. In principle, at least. But I'm still a bit worried. So far everything you have told me is going to increase our estimate. We're already over budget, and I'm no longer convinced that we have considered the risks in anything like enough detail."

"It's not the detail that matters," Larry said. "It's more to do with your general approach to risk. But before we look at sources of risk, can I ask you how you came up with the figures in your *basic* estimate?"

It was a simple enough question, and I felt quite happy to be giving *him* a lesson for a change.

"Well, first we break the whole job into phases and then into major achievements. We call these milestones. Next we consider each milestone in turn. Whoever in the team has the most expertise takes responsibility for planning, estimating and organising that part of the job, although they may need help from the rest of us on some aspects. The estimate itself is mainly based on experience, of course, and for the more complex milestones we often break the work down into smaller chunks. We call them work packages. For some we have to get quotations from suppliers. Others we estimate ourselves."

"Yes, but how?" Larry asked again.

"I've already told you. Experience," I said.

"Yes, but *how* do you use your experience?" he insisted.

I still didn't see the trap.

"Well, I suppose where we know a job is urgent we go for the quickest way of doing it and use our experience to estimate how many people will need to work for how many hours and how much they will spend on materials and so on. Then we multiply the hours by the cost per hour – the labour plus overhead rate – and add everything up to get our initial cost estimate."

Larry looked thoughtful. "Does it work?" he asked.

I was tempted to ask him to explain what he meant, but in truth I knew the answer. He meant do we get our estimates right? I shook my head.

"Have you ever got an estimate wildly wrong?" he asked.

I told him about a rushed quotation we did for Unicomtech, where we accidentally multiplied the materials cost by the labour rate. The trouble was, with such a mass of figures and so little time to check everything, nobody noticed. We lost that job on price. The really annoying thing is, we would have won easily if we hadn't messed up the estimate.

"I think you are missing an opportunity," he told me. "Especially in the high-risk parts of the job."

"OK, explain," I said.

"Better still," he replied, "let's try an example. See that building over there?"

"The boiler house?" I asked.

"Yes. Supposing we could cut it away from its foundations at ground level and then weigh it. Just the building – forget the boiler. How heavy is it, would you say?"

"No idea," I said. "I'm not a surveyor, nor a builder."

"Go on – try," Larry insisted. "Give me the best answer you can come up with in two minutes."

I took up pencil and paper.

The building was about ten feet long and eight wide, with a flat roof about nine feet above the ground. It was brick-built, with just one small window. A pair of double doors took up most of one end. I thought I might just be able to lift one of the doors, so I wrote down 200 lb for the pair of doors. The window I guessed was no more than 50 lb.

"Time's up!" Larry said. "What have you got?"

I showed him my scribble pad.

"Two or three hundred pounds, then. Is that it?" Larry asked.

"No. I mean, the walls must weigh tons and tons. And the roof. Give me another minute. There must be getting on for three hundred square yards of walling, and say it's about a foot thick ..." – I did a quick sum – "I make it about eighty cubic yards of stonework at – let's say two tons per cubic yard. So that's – a hundred and sixty tons. The roof is mainly wood, so that can't weigh much. I'd say the total is around a hundred and seventy tons," I said.

I felt quite pleased with myself after all that.

"Good," Larry said. "Now do it another way. Any other way you please."

"I can't see that there *is* another way," I told him.

"OK. Let's suppose you wanted to build a second boiler house, identical to that one. The materials are all delivered by builder's trucks. How many full loads?"

I closed my eyes and pictured a truck loaded with bricks and timber.

"That's odd," I told him. "I reckon we could get everything in a single load. Two at the most."

"An average truck of the type we're talking about can carry something like twenty tons. The biggest ones hold nearly double that," Larry said. "How does your a hundred and seventy tons sound now?"

"Miles out," I said.

"Not much of an *estimate*," Larry jibed. "Now then, supposing you were to smash down the boiler house. How many rubbish skips would you fill in clearing up all the rubble? Half a dozen, maybe?" I nodded. "A builders' skip holds around four tons of rubble."

"I see. So where did I go wrong in my first estimate?" I asked.

"I think you'll find there are nearer twenty-seven square yards of walling than two hundred and seventy," he said.

I checked through my calculations. Sure enough, Larry was right: in my haste I had accidentally slipped the decimal point one place to the right.

"Mistakes like that are easily made," he said. "But the big opportunity you missed was to cross-check. If you only do your estimates one way you are far less likely to spot a serious mistake. In particular, it's always advisable to estimate any high-risk work in more than one way."

Always estimate high-risk work using more than one method

"That's a really useful tip," I said. "I wish I'd known about it when we were doing the Unicomtech bid. Still, it's not too late for the Bilston job. We haven't finalised the estimates yet."

This seemed a good point to take a break, and I went to see whether anything had come in from Bilstons in the mail.

When I got back, I found that Larry had summarised the key points on a flipchart, and I said I would get it typed up so the whole team could have a copy:

- ◆ Estimates need to take account of uncertainty
- ◆ Plans also need to take account of risks
- ◆ Components of an estimate:

  - Well-defined work
  - Ill-defined work (including dealing with interruptions)
  - Rework (due to mistakes)
  - Funds for dealing with risks

- ◆ Estimating high-risk work

  - Use two or more methods
  - Cross-check between the results of each method

"Before we leave this subject, there's just one more thing," Larry said. "I'm pretty sure you will find that most of the big opportunities are contained in the risky parts of the job. So, looking at the risks from more than one viewpoint can provide you with an additional advantage. You are more likely to find hidden opportunities."

Looking at risks from several viewpoints can help expose hidden opportunities

I wanted to ask lots more questions, such as how you actually go about finding opportunities within risks, but Larry said it would be better to concentrate on understanding risks first of all.

Next, Larry and I talked about typical sources of risk, and I could see immediately that just about all of them occurred in our kind of work. Some were dependent on random uncertainties such as the weather, and would lead to outcomes spread either side of the norm. Others, like the opening or non-opening of a parachute, could go one way or another; they depended more on events that could, as Larry termed it, 'alter the course of Destiny, like splits in the fabric of time'.

In next to no time we came up with quite a catalogue of risks, but they all fell into one of three categories: they were related either to people, to the work itself, or to the environment in which the work is carried out. This latter category is more than just the physical environment; it also has commercial, political, economic and social aspects.

Major sources of risk:

- the people
- the work
- the environment

People are a major source of all kinds of risk. In many cases, you can't be sure in advance who will do a particular piece of work, and yet people's ability, pace of working and thoroughness vary considerably. Some people are reasonably steady in their performance, while others are far more erratic. (My own off days are poor value, by any standards.) It is also important to remember that most people's enthusiasm tends to wax and wane, and motivation can have a big effect on performance.

Apart from the general randomness of individual effectiveness, there are plenty of other risks. People make mistakes, and rarely are these predictable. Experience suggests it is unwise to assume that things will only go wrong in the 'difficult' parts of a job; often a crucial step gets missed out in a relatively straightforward task either because people have become complacent or are bored with the unchallenging nature of the work.

Mistakes are rarely predictable; even easy jobs can go wrong

Then somebody gets a shirt with no collar, a book with a chapter missing, a pie with no filling. If a worker proves to be not as competent as at first you thought they were, you might have to take them off real work and provide extra training; that means even more delay and extra cost.

But there are also risks in having extremely able people working on a job. They are highly sought after, and at a crucial time a key player might decide to leave; then someone else has to step in and try to fill the gap. The disruption not only affects progress on that one important aspect of the work, but it also tends to demoralise the rest of the team and so other parts of the job can suffer delays, too.

Resistance to change is a difficult problem to overcome. You may work for many months defining, devising and fine-tuning a better way of doing things. You roll out your change initiative amid a great fanfare and you spend vast amounts of time and money on communication and training only to find, a few months later, that people have reverted to 'the old way'. And why? Because they understand the old way better and they felt threatened by the change. Some call it bloody-mindedness; others say that without a shared vision and a belief in the new way any change is bound to be unsustainable. In due course, hindsight will tell us whether we got it right; foresight can only penetrate so far through the fog.

In time, hindsight will tell us how far our foresight penetrated the fog of the future

The people who actually do the work are not the only ones whose performance affects progress. One of the greatest risks in long-term work of any sort is that the initial support and commitment of senior management might not be sustained through the life of the job. It is standing room only in the state of 'Top Priority' where King Fickleness rules. Every new job becomes top priority until the unblessed commit themselves to the targets; then the moving finger writes large for someone else.

One of the greatest risks in long-term jobs is that senior management commitment might evaporate

It is always more difficult to hold a team together when the ultimate goal is many months or even years away, but, if the necessary resources and facilities to do the job are promised and then not delivered, people can lose heart. How many estimates are based on the assumption that the work will be done by dispirited people?

Few estimates presume the work will be done by dispirited people

Whenever you have to depend on other people you are taking a risk. They may show concern for your well-being and for the success of what you are trying to do, but when the going gets tough you will probably find that they care even more deeply about their own survival and their own comfort. Selfishness is a survival instinct. Without this trait mankind would long ago have become extinct.

Selfishness is a survival instinct – any totally unselfish creatures are already extinct

Even at the best of times clients and customers, suppliers and subcontractors are not entirely rational: such organisations are, after all, staffed by people vulnerable to the foibles of human nature. And at the worst of times any organisation can seem like a mindless machine into whose works mindless people thrash around like random spanners tossed at the whim of Chance. Rarely is the whole thing entirely chaotic, but on the other hand no amount of planning and foresight will ever make it entirely pre-dictable. Problem people are the only kind of people there are.

Problem people are the only kind of people

The work itself is another source of uncertainty and risk. For one thing, we plan and estimate the work at a time when we know least about it. There are often parts of the job where we don't understand exactly what we will need to do and we have even less idea how to do it. It is equally risky to assume that the customer's knowledge of the requirement is complete and accurate.

It is folly to assume that the customer's knowledge of the requirement is complete and accurate

Sometimes we have to redo work as the fog clears and we begin to understand the true requirements. And then there are also risks related to new or unfamiliar technology and new and unproven processes and techniques; this can mean that some very fine work is destroyed or has to be scrapped because of failures later on in the process.

The more innovation a job demands, the more difficult it is to deploy and coordinate a large team. And how do you predict how long it will take to make a breakthrough?

Predicting the unpredictable is a risky business

The creative elements of a job are, by definition, risky; indeed, some targets may prove unattainable. Then it is not merely a matter of exceeding budget and overrunning the schedule: the requirement has to be amended to something that is achievable. Or you may have to cancel the job altogether. This would lead to a future very different from the one foreseen at the outset.

Assumptions are dangerous creatures. They need handling with care. The most venomous species are implicit assumptions; often they conceal the most terrible risks.

On one thing Larry and I were totally united: all assumptions should be put down at birth. Put down in writing. Then, Larry suggested, it helps if each person in the team says, in their own words, what they think the written assumption really means. Surprisingly, perhaps, even written assumptions can mean different things to different people.

Assumptions are monsters: they should be put down at birth – in writing

What you are setting out to achieve might be critically dependent on some other work going on in parallel and providing you with resources or essential information. Equally, your own achievements may be drivers to other jobs that will be adversely affected if you fail to meet your targets. Sometimes a more serious risk is that the technical requirements of one or other of these dependent tasks may change without this fact being revealed to those involved in the other work. Only when everything comes together are the communication failures evident, and by then you may have a crisis on your hands.

Linked activities of this type are areas of high risk; like babies, they need continual attention at both ends.

Communication links are like babies: they need continual care and attention at both ends

People don't work in a vacuum, of course. The environment is essential. It is a life-support system. As a source of risk, therefore, the environment in all its aspects – technical, physical, psychological, social, commercial, financial and political – demands continual attention.

The working environment can be a very dangerous place. It is a major risk area, and managing risks to the physical safety and well-being of people at work is an important duty of every manager. From lifting accidents to repetitive strain injuries, there is no end of risks to people at work. Reducing the likelihood and if possible the consequences of such risks is second nature to some managers; others take a more cavalier attitude and so, whether an accident occurs or not, they risk losing the commitment of their staff. There are also physical risks to equipment and products. We ignore these at our peril, too.

Larry made a big issue of the psychological environment and its impact on team effectiveness. He said that the value of a meeting was probably as much determined by the atmosphere created by whoever chaired the meeting as it was by the expertise of those attending.

"Why do you say that?" I asked.

"Because atmosphere affects behaviour," he replied. "For example, it's hard to take people seriously when they are continually cracking jokes or making flippant remarks. It's also difficult to concentrate on a complicated problem when you are forever being distracted by interruptions or noise. And just try thinking creatively with someone yelling, *'Hurry up, for heaven's sake. We haven't got all day.'* What chance then?"

"Point taken," I said.

We went on to discuss the risks inherent in the commercial,

social and political environments. Some markets are very fickle, and things can quickly come in and go out of fashion. (Who could have predicted the impact on the Swiss watch industry of the invention of the digital electronic watch?) The level of competition, especially from abroad, isn't easy to predict, and prophesying the future actions of competitors is a particularly dodgy game. Changes in local, national and international regulations are also sources of risk; they can sweep aside the most reasoned of forecasts.

A day can be a very long time in international politics. Many a successful export business has foundered overnight as, following a change of government, their political acceptability as a supplier has been overturned and competitors from a more favoured country have captured the market. It's all very well to talk of spreading the risk, but with the kinds of products and services that are linked closely to national cultures that isn't always possible.

At this point Larry called another break. (We were both ready for one.) This time *I* prepared the flipchart summary:

Sources of risk

◆ People:
- – unpredictable and error-prone
- – resistant to change
- – top-level commitment can evaporate

◆ The work itself:
- – poorly understood when planning
- – unproven techniques/processes
- – breakthroughs not available on demand
- – assumptions are monsters
- – links to and dependence upon other jobs

◆ The environment:
- – technical/physical
- – psychological/social
- – commercial/financial
- – political

All the things we had been talking about are just headings under which we can often find risks. On some jobs a particular heading might be relevant; on others maybe not. But lists like this are no substitute for thought. As Larry said: "In every new job there will also be new risks of a kind that you have never had to deal with before – that's part of the nature of change. It is also a major source of new opportunity."

Risks of a kind you have never had to deal with before are a major source of opportunity

After the break, we went on to consider the likely effect of the risks.

"What we do," Larry said, "rather as you have done, is to list the things we are trying to achieve and what we think we will have to do to fulfil those aims. Alongside all this we can then make a list of the risks we can foresee."

"Let's see if I've got this right," I said. "Rather than allocating some notional contingency, you list the *actual risks* in the work to be done. Is that it?" I asked.

"That's what we *try* to do. But remember, risks aren't necessarily inherent in the objectives themselves, but more often in the way you decide to achieve those objectives. For example, if surveying a crocodile-infested swamp is your objective, the size of boat you use will determine the level of risk. Surveying the swamp without using a boat might be the low-cost option, but it would carry a high risk."

"I see what you mean," I said, uncurling my toes.

Larry told me that in practice, when we try to foresee the risks, inevitably we get some of them right and some wrong. And we are bound to miss quite a few, no matter how hard we try.

"Why don't you have a go at listing the main risks on this Bilston job?" he suggested. "You get that done and then I'll show you how to make a better risk-management plan."

All the while Larry had been talking, my confidence in our draft plan had been falling. It had now reached ground level. I tore it up, there and then: the parachute had not opened. The only thing I knew for certain was that I couldn't afford to risk using our present plan.

"OK," I sighed. "So we need to list any risks that we think might limit our ability to carry out each task successfully, and then consider the consequences of each risk. Right?"

Larry nodded. He said that where you cannot reasonably forecast the precise impact of a risk in terms of reduced quality, increased cost, extended timescale or whatever, you could still rank it as a high, medium or low impact. And in the same way you can make a judgement on the likelihood of the risk occurring. Some people use high, medium and low, while others try to guess at the percentages. Larry agreed with our practice of using 1 per cent for low probability, 5 per cent for moderate probability and 50 per cent for risks rated as having a high probability of occurring, although he did say that where you have the necessary experience you should try to use more precise figures.

On some of our jobs there were probably enough historical data available on computer to allow us to do this, although it seemed to me that a lot would depend on the type of work involved. In commissioning a deep-sea drilling rig or launching a communications satellite, it would be crazy to ignore statistical data on weather conditions. I checked this out with Larry, suggesting that where we have access to statistical information on failure rates we could put the historical percentages into the plan.

"Sure. That's often a sound approach," he said. "Unless, of course, you are aware of other factors that will raise or lower the risk in your particular case."

We went on to discuss the second step in the risk assessment. (That's what we were really talking about, I realised.) Here, Larry told me, you need to consider in turn the effects of each risk becoming reality – the loss or damage you would sustain.

This might be schedule slip, a performance or quality defect, a cost overrun, loss of staff morale, a disgruntled customer – perhaps all of these. Maybe something else. Where possible, you try to estimate the size of the loss. With schedule slip and cost overrun the answer will be a number. For other types of loss, such as customer confidence, which are not easily quantified, you can still assess the impact of the risk but you have to use a subjective scale such as high, medium and low.

Ultimately, of course, all these problems come home to roost as reduced profit on the contract *and* a failure to win profitable follow-on orders. So you have to find new customers, and that means increased sales and marketing costs, and therefore a less profitable business in the future.

So now you can work out the seriousness of each risk – what Larry called the level of risk exposure – by multiplying the impact by the probability of it occurring. He said you can think of this as the amount of bad luck you could expect if you went ahead ignoring the risks.

Risk exposure is the product of the impact of an event and its probability of occurrence

"So are the most serious risks the ones giving the greatest exposure?" I asked.

"Generally, yes, but not always," Larry replied. "Statistically, I suppose they should be. But another key factor, human perception of risk, is being ignored in these simple calculations. You can't always get away with ignoring perception. People often give disproportionate weighting to the consequences of risk, especially when the consequences are frightening."

Larry explained what he meant by perception. He said that if the impact of a risk is unacceptably high and there is any way of reducing it, people will often spend far more in mitigating the risk than could be justified purely on the basis of the calculated exposure.

People often spend far more on mitigating a risk than is justified purely on the basis of the calculated risk exposure

I told him that was about as clear as mud.

"OK," he said. "Let's say there is a 10 per cent chance of you losing a thousand pounds this year. What is the maximum amount you would consider spending to reduce that chance to zero?"

"Ten per cent of a thousand pounds is – one hundred pounds," I said. "That would be the average impact of the loss. So if I spent more than one hundred pounds, and made lots of such decisions, I would on average be paying out more than it was worth."

"Good," Larry said. "Now add two zeros and try it again."

"What do you mean?" I asked.

"Let's say your home is worth a hundred thousand pounds and the chance is one in a thousand that it will be destroyed by fire this year. Your risk exposure is still one hundred pounds. Would you refuse to insure it if the premium came to over one hundred pounds?"

My house wasn't quite in that price bracket, and yet my insurance premium was much higher than a hundred pounds (although the policy did cover a few other minor risks as well as fire).

"Your perception of the risk is now greater," Larry went on. "This is because in the worst case you would lose your home, and you are willing to pay more than the value of the risk exposure to avoid that risk. Insurance companies can only stay in business while perception influences people's judgement of the level of risk they are exposed to."

Larry said that there are many instances where people will accept a higher target price or a later delivery date provided they perceive that the uncertainty surrounding the final price or the actual delivery date is relatively small. Uncertainty can make people feel anxious; a reduction in uncertainty is sometimes worth more to them than a reduction in the mean cost.

A reduction in uncertainty is often perceived as worth more than a reduction in the mean cost

I could see that this perception factor is not entirely rational. Some people are so concerned at the risks of air travel that they refuse to travel by plane. They would rather make a two-day car journey than spend just two hours travelling by plane. The risk exposure is greater when travelling by road, but many people perceive the risk as lower. This might be partly because they feel they have no control of the situation if they travel by air and partly because they expect the consequences to be greater in an air crash. (And yet the very same people may continue smoking cigarettes, even though medical experts tell them that a heavy smoker's life expectancy is ten years shorter than that of non-smokers. Where's the logic in that?)

Larry told me that when you don't have the ability or the resources to mitigate every risk, you sometimes do need to take perception into account when deciding which risks will receive priority for mitigation.

When you cannot mitigate every risk, perception may have to influence your priorities

"I see," I said. "So, because of this perception factor, reducing the impact of a risk is better than reducing its likelihood of occurrence. Is that it?"

"It can be, yes," he said vaguely. "But there is more to it than that. Do you remember I said that the spread of a risk – the range over which the outcome might vary – is often perceived as more important than the magnitude of the risk? Being able to predict accurately when something will be completed is sometimes perceived as being more valuable than making a moderate 'probable' saving in time but with a wide range of possible completion dates. This means that a low-impact risk with a high likelihood of occurrence is generally more acceptable than a high-impact risk with a low probability of occurrence, even though both might give the same calculated risk exposure."

A low-impact risk with a high likelihood of occurrence is generally more acceptable than a high-impact risk with a low probability of occurrence

Larry explained that impact mitigation – reducing the loss you would suffer if a risk should become reality – isn't always possible. He went back to the air-travel analogy to illustrate the point.

Air safety has improved enormously in recent times, mainly because the planes are so much more reliable and monitoring systems give early warning of most kinds of problems; but, on the rare occasions that a plane does crash, the chances of survival are still not very great. Some people worry a lot about that.

With a world population of five billion people, two or three thousand air-crash fatalities a year amounts to each person facing one chance in two million of losing something like forty years off their life. So on average each person on the planet loses no more than two minutes of their life per year due to air-crash fatality. Over an eighty-year lifetime, this adds up to just three hours off the average person's life-span.

It's pretty obvious that road travel has the edge as far as perception is concerned. There are many more crashes and many more people are killed. In effect road travel takes several months off the average human life-span. But a smaller *proportion* of the crashes are fatal, and some people are influenced unduly by that.

"I can quite understand people worrying about things that can kill them," I said.

Larry chuckled. "I'd sooner travel by air, any day," he said. "The view is heavenly up there, and the risk exposure is a hell of a lot lower."

"OK, so what do I do about this perception factor?" I asked.

"All I'm saying," he replied, "is that because of the perception factor you may have to modify your view of the relative importance of some risks. In most cases, perhaps you won't. But just be aware of the possibility."

I decided to stick with the simple risk-exposure calculation and see if I could make any sense of that. I could see that a 10 per cent probability of spending an extra ten thousand pounds on a job means that the risk exposure is one thousand pounds. Similarly, a 20 per cent probability of slipping five weeks suggests a risk exposure of one week of schedule slippage. But none of this made me feel happy. All these calculations would take time: time we simply couldn't afford to waste. And it wasn't as if it was going to make the job any easier – at least, not as far as I could see. The whole thing seemed much too complicated to manage on a day-to-day basis. I needed some-thing much simpler. I was about to say so when Larry pulled out another of his charts.

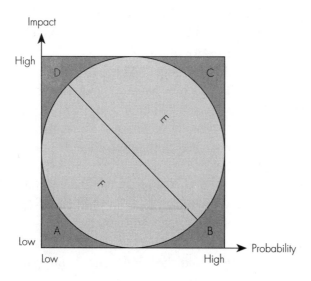

"It's quite simple, actually," he said. "Whether you bother with numbers or not, this is what it's really all about. This is a risk-prioritisation chart. Its purpose is to help you decide how to manage each of the risks."

"Oh no," I groaned. "There is nothing I hate more than graphs, charts and fancy diagrams that claim to show me how simple my job is. Or how simple I am for not understanding them. Often all they do is make simple or irrelevant ideas look sophisticated and clever. If it's that complicated let's forget it, Larry. This stuff is far too bureaucratic for me and my people."

Larry stared at me as though I had just arrived from another planet. His silent criticism had the desired effect: I got rattled.

"Anyway, how can *your* chart possibly tell me what to do to manage any of *my* risks?" I retorted.

Larry didn't throw a tantrum. He didn't walk off as I might have done. But he did look decidedly uncomfortable. "I can understand you feeling that way," he said, "but what I actually said was that this chart can help you decide *how* to manage risks. It's your job to decide *what to do*. No chart can tell you that. But let me ask you a question: how do you decide whether a risk deserves proactive management or reactive management?"

"Hang on a minute, Larry," I said. "That's exactly why I need your help. Tell me about this proactive and reactive stuff. We don't do any of that in my department."

"I'll bet you do," Larry said. "Although perhaps you don't recognise it as such. Tell me, have you got any machinery in your factory?"

"Some," I said. "A couple of presses. Some lathes. Oh yes, and a numerically controlled milling machine. Is that the sort of thing you had in mind?"

"Yes. Now then, do your operators have any training before they get to use the machinery?" I nodded. "And how about safety? Are the machines fitted with guards?"

"Of course," I told him.

"Right! The training and the safety guards are part of your

proactive risk-management plan. And do you ever have to call upon a first aider to patch up a cut or a bruise?"

"Not often. Our safety record is very good, actually. We're proud of it. But we do have the occasional mishap. Every firm does. Usually when someone gets careless. Mind you, I remember the time a lathe tool shattered. Chunks of steel smashed right through the safety guard. That was something neither we nor the lathe manufacturer had thought possible. One of the operators got a nasty gash on the forehead. He was lucky – he could easily have lost an eye. Naturally, we had tougher safety guards fitted right away. As far as I know we've had no problems since."

"All right! Well, your first-aid staff are part of your reactive risk management – your contingency plan for dealing with the occasional crisis, such as the case you mentioned. So you see, you are already using both proactive and reactive risk management, rather than dealing with *all* problems by crisis management."

"I see," I said. "So these principles apply to all our work. To the continuous business-as-usual stuff as well as to the special assignments and projects. Yes?"

Larry nodded. He told me that in his department they have an ongoing improvement programme – a set of internal assignments where they act as both the customer and the supplier. The aim is to improve the risk management of their day-to-day activities. It has already helped them to cut costs and boost their profits quite a bit. The alternative, he suggested, is a life of chaos. I knew all about that. There's nothing worse than a succession of unexpected crises for throwing every other planned activity off course.

> ### There's nothing worse than a succession of unexpected crises for throwing plans off course

In a business that relies on seat-of-pants planning – the wait-and-see syndrome – people are continually being diverted from one emergency to another. This, I was well aware, is just about the most inefficient way of using resources.

Wait-and-see management is the least efficient way of using resources

Larry had his own way of putting it: "Just imagine what your factory would be like if you let untrained people loose on those machines!"

"It doesn't bear thinking about," I told him. "It would be murder."

"So why run the rest of your work that way?" he asked.

"Er, I've changed my mind, Larry," I told him. "I think you had better explain the chart."

Larry grinned. He explained that every one of our risks could be mapped on to the chart. The position of a risk will depend on the probability of the risk occurring and on the seriousness of its consequences.

That I could understand, and so I let Larry go into the details.

"Look at the region marked A," he said. "Any risk in this region is very unlikely to happen and its impact, in comparison with the whole job, is also very small. How serious would it be if you ignored such a risk?"

"I can't honestly see that it would matter a jot," I replied.

"I agree. In most cases you can ignore risks that map into this region and concentrate your attention on the others."

"That's useful," I told him. "It must help to cut the list down to a more manageable size."

Larry nodded. "Now let's look at region B," he said. "Any risk in this sector is not going to have much of an effect, but it is quite likely to occur. What now?"

"Ignore it?" I offered.

"You could," he said. "But a better way might be to build in to your basic estimate the money and resources you think you will need to deal with it. Then you can assume that it is going to happen and forget all about it unless it does."

"But wouldn't that put *up* the costs of the work? And anyway, I thought ignoring problems that are likely to happen was the hallmark of bad management."

Myth
It is bad management to ignore
problems

"Yes, it will put up costs. But not a lot. And don't forget that managing problems takes time, and your time costs money, too. In many instances ignoring these minor problems can free up a lot of management time. Bad management is being too busy dealing with trivial issues to do the important things really well."

It is bad management to let trivia
deflect attention from serious
issues

"Point taken," I agreed. "So what about region C, extremely serious consequences and very likely to occur? How do I manage that sort of risk?"

"You don't," he told me. "Not if you've got any sense."

"But surely," I said, "if we ignore these sorts of risks we could get into serious difficulties."

"It's worse than that," Larry said. "If you take these sorts of risks your outfit will soon get into very deep trouble and you will *almost certainly go broke*. When you are in the risk business you should expect to make reasonable profits that are related to the level of risk. You would need to make *unreasonable* profits if you wanted to cover unreasonably high risks, and that would mean charging unreasonable prices. And since there's no reason why customers should pay unreasonable prices, what you have to do is find a way of getting the job done without involving these unacceptably high levels of risk exposure."

Some risks are not worth worrying about; others are not worth contemplating

"Yes, but how?" I asked.

"Let me give you an example," Larry said. "In your opinion would most people consider crossing the Niagara Falls in an aeroplane to be an acceptable risk?"

"I guess so, if they were with a qualified pilot."

"OK. And how about crossing on a tightrope?" he asked.

"Not for me, thank you. For some people, maybe. Tightrope experts. Yes, I guess it might be acceptable. But they probably wouldn't do it unless someone was going to pay them a hell of a lot of money."

"Right. But now how about trying it *without* the tightrope?"

"Point taken," I said. "That would be suicide. All right, I've got the message about unreasonable risk."

Something was still bothering me about all this. There were some serious risks on the Bilston job, and I was pretty sure there was no way of avoiding them.

"So what about region D?" I asked. "There the consequences are just as high even though the probability is low. But if one of those risks ever became reality the business would suffer just as much damage as in the previous case."

"I wouldn't worry too much about that if I were you," Larry replied.

"Don't worry about something that might cripple the business? Why on earth not?" I asked.

"Because in most cases you will probably find that there's nothing you can afford to do about it. I mean, just suppose there was an earthquake and this factory disappeared into a hole in the ground. Would you still be able to deliver on time against the Bilston contract?"

"No chance!" I told him.

"Then why aren't you building in a one hundred per cent cost contingency so that you can do the job twice, once here and once in our Rochester plant? OK, you don't have to answer that. It's because your price would be miles out of court and you wouldn't stand the slightest chance of winning the contract. Agreed?"

Some low-probability high-consequence risks are unavoidable; you just have to live with them

"Agreed!" I replied. "You've made your point."

What Larry was really saying was that I should avoid unnecessary risks in area D, and reduce or mitigate any risks where the cost of mitigation is affordable, but that I would have to accept and learn to live with some very low-probability risks whose impact can't reasonably be mitigated.

Next we turned our attention to the circle in the middle of the chart. Larry said that in practice this is where thorough planning gives the biggest pay-off. He explained that where the product of the impact and the probability is fairly high – a result falling into region E – it's usually best to devise some form of proactive risk-management plan, at least sufficient to reduce the exposure and push it into region F, if not right down into region A where you can afford to ignore it.

"Oh, I see," I said, freewheeling. Then I put my brain into gear. "No, I don't see. You'll have to go through that in a bit more detail, Larry. This really is quite complicated stuff. How about showing me an example?"

"It's not really difficult. So far, all you have had to do is to consider two aspects of a risk, the impact and the probability, so that you can mark its position on the chart. The clever bit is working out how you are going to *manage* the risk. I've got some guidelines to help you set priorities for doing that. Like a copy?"

"You bet," I said. I needed all the help I could get.

Larry's priority-setting guidelines were simple enough. They consisted of a marked-up copy of the risk chart.

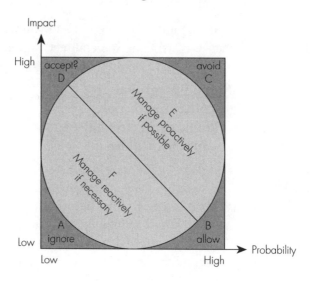

He explained that for the higher-risk exposures, those in region E, you would try to find an initiative that could either eliminate the risk altogether or at least mitigate it to the point where any further reduction in risk exposure would cost more than you would save.

"I think I get it," I told him. "If it takes a fortnight to avoid a risk exposure of a week, then clearly it's better simply to take the risk."

"Yes, usually," Larry agreed.

"You mean unless the perception was that the risk had to be avoided at all costs," I said.

Larry nodded. "Yes. That's right. But in practice you will also have to manage some risks reactively. I've shown these as region F on the chart. The position of the dividing line between regions E and F will depend on how much resource you have available for proactive management. It will also depend on the nature of the job itself, of course. Some risks cannot be reduced to zero no matter how much resource you apply to them, and so the residual risk will still have to be managed reactively."

At last I felt I understood the basic principles. I could get the team together and map out the risks on the Bilston job.

"When is the best time to make the risk-management plans?" I asked.

"Generally, the earlier you plan your proactive measures the better, for two reasons," Larry replied. "Firstly, your freedom to manoeuvre reduces with time. What I mean is that as time goes by the number of counter-measure options available to you will reduce. If you wait too long, some of the risks become reality and you are left with only the reactive-management options."

If you wait too long, risks become reality and you are left with only reactive-management options

"But there is a second reason," Larry went on. "You will also want to look at opportunity management right from the outset. That's because, as time goes by and risks become reality, opportunities can also fade away."

Now that I *could* understand. But what I could *not* yet see was how it could be worth making reactive-management plans in advance – planning the panics, so to speak. I asked Larry how he would deal with these kinds of risks.

"These are simply your contingency plans," Larry said. "It's usually worth mapping out in broad terms how you would deal with some of the more significant risks, but otherwise I would say look in detail only at the next two or three months. At the lower levels of risk exposure the longer-term picture is often pretty confused, so as the work proceeds you will need to review your contingency plans. At the same time, of course, be on the lookout for copycat opportunities and windfalls. Reactive opportunity management can usually be linked to reactive risk management, you will find."

Reactive opportunity management can usually be linked to reactive risk management

This seemed a natural place to stop. Again, with Larry's help, I drew up a flipchart summary of the key points from our final session:

♦   Assess actual risks, not merely risk areas
♦   Map the risks

   –   impact
   –   probability

♦   Avoid options involving unnecessary or unacceptable risks
♦   Use the risk map to set general priorities
♦   Modify priorities where customer/public perception is a factor

---

Larry suggested that I should go through my basic plan for the Bilston job and list the risks, categorising them using the risk chart, and then decide on the best way to manage each major risk.

I would need to get the team together and brainstorm alternative ways of dealing with each major risk. It wouldn't be a five-minute job, but by the time we had done all that I reckoned we ought to have a much better understanding of what the Bilston job was likely to throw at us.

It had cost me nearly half a day, but all this had given me a better idea of what sort of information ought to be in my plan, even though I still hadn't much of a clue what the plan would look like and how we would use it to manage risk and opportunity.

Still one step at a time. Lots of ideas were beginning to take shape. With another weekend looming, this seemed a good time to bring my opportunity-management notebook up to date.

Risk: its identifying features, habitat and behaviour

- When things go better than expected, you can gain a little time; when things go badly, you can lose a lot more.
- All risks eventually resolve – as opportunities dissolve.
- Some risks resolve gradually with advancing time, as more information becomes available; other risks are more like forks in the road to the future.
- Technological and business-process change, task complexity, the working environment, and the unpredictability of people are all sources of risk.
- Some risks can be ignored; others cannot be avoided.
- Some risks are trivial and not worth worrying about; others are so serious that accepting them should not be contemplated.
- Risks can be described by their impact – cost, time or other forms of loss – and the likelihood of the risk becoming reality.
- Risk exposure is the product of the impact of a risk if it occurs and the likelihood of it occurring.
- People's perception of individual risk is sometimes a factor in setting priorities for managing them.
- Where possible, it is wise to take initiatives to reduce high-risk exposures; lower exposures may have to be dealt with reactively should they materialise.
- A reduction in uncertainty is often perceived as worth more than a reduction in the mean cost.
- It's important not to let a plethora of trivial uncertainties deflect you from managing the most serious risks.

Action: I must learn how to plan for managing risks.

Chapter 5

The hunting of the unicorn: in search of opportunity

Jean would never admit it, but she hadn't a clue what Bilstons would want to see or what the chief executive expected. She would have signed off my plan without question if I had said that I had halved the engineers' estimates. With hindsight it would have been better to have involved her earlier: I had been putting it off, and now I was going to regret it.

In the end, on Monday morning I simply handed her the figures and waited for the inevitable barrage of questions and criticism.

"Is this going to be cost-competitive? As far as I can see it doesn't seem to stack up with Bilstons' budget." I put on my impassive face (I'm told it's actually a frown). "Technically, I leave the whole thing to you, Jim. You know that. But on the costing side I need evidence that you know what you're doing. And at present I'm far from convinced." She picked up a printout file and let it drop dismissively onto the desk between us. "This engineering estimate is a non-starter in any case. It's way over the target. The board will throw it out, I can assure you."

"OK, have it your way," I snapped angrily. (I have always resented being spoken to like a child, especially when I am being childish.) "You tell me the answer and I'll pretend it's my estimate. But remember, Jean, I've already given you the best advice I can on what it will cost us to do the job, so don't blame me later if you hear that we're making a cracking loss on the deal."

Jean looked worried. "No, Jim. They are your estimates. You've got to decide. But I do need to be convinced that you can do the job within a realistic budget. You must understand that."

She stood up, her chair scraping on the polished floor with a rumble of thunder. Dark clouds crossed her face and lightning flashed in her green eyes. I thought she was going to storm out in a rage, and the way I was feeling I would have enjoyed that. But instead she picked up my estimates, thrust them at me, and said calmly: "Find 15 per cent by next Wednesday week. If you don't, we can't win the contract. All our market intelligence tells us we need to go in below Bilstons' budget, and the chief won't let us bid this one at a loss. By the end of next week Gilbert Manning wants to review the figures. And, as you know, we need to get our bid to Bilstons a week after that. So – 15 per cent. It's not negotiable, Jim."

I stormed out, slamming the door behind me.

Jean's new secretary was struggling to stifle a giggle. (She was just a kid.)

It was time for me to stop being childish, too. Jean was right. Somehow we had to cut costs without downgrading the specification. There was no point in offering Bilstons something they didn't want. The exam question was set, and my job was to come up with a better answer than any of our competitors: I had to bridge the gap between our estimate and the target that Jean and the marketing people had come up with. But how?

Not by shouting my mouth off at Jean; that was for sure.

I retraced my steps, opened her door and peered in. "Sorry!" I said. "Leave it with me and I'll see what I can do."

"Sure, Jim. I know you will," she said with a cheerful smile. "A week on Wednesday, then. Fifteen per cent. Right?" I nodded, and left her punching data into a spreadsheet.

Now that we were getting a clearer view of the risks involved in the Bilston job, I phoned Larry to ask how I should go about opportunity planning. It was Tuesday, and we had just seven working days to get the numbers Jean needed. By this time I was feeling pretty miserable: after two extremely heated cost-review meetings our estimate was still way above what Marketing said would be necessary for a winning bid. We also needed to pull back the delivery schedule by a couple of months, and that, in my experience, was likely to push costs up further – just what we did not need. In other words, we were in desperate need of something not far short of a miracle. Deep down I felt sure that opportunity management could help achieve cost and schedule savings. I had no idea what to do about it – but I knew a man who did. Unfortunately *he* had been away visiting a client in Germany and wouldn't be back at work until the following morning.

When, eventually, I got through to Larry in Munich, he could only spare me a couple of minutes.

"First decide what to put into your wish list," he told me. "Then find or create opportunities and prepare a plan to take advantage of them. Finally, make your wishes come true by exploiting the opportunities. It's a simple enough process. Much like any other management job, really."

As simple as that, eh? Well, getting started would be no problem. I knew how much I needed to cut from our cost estimates and how much time I needed to save – I had my wish list. But the rest wasn't going to be so easy. What I did *not* have was a list of opportunities. None had fallen from the sky in the last few days; I didn't know where to look; and as for creating opportunities, I hadn't a clue how to go about it. On the plus side, the risk list looked reasonably comprehensive and the team had seemed fairly happy with the work schedule – that is until I told them how much time and money we needed to slash off the estimates. Then, predictably, they had thrown their hands up in horror. I only averted a mutiny by suggesting we should all get together to brainstorm an opportunity-management plan.

Thinking about it, I realised that things weren't as black as all that. They were a strong team, bright people, very committed. Given the chance, they could be creative. I didn't have to have all the ideas myself. Good teamwork, I convinced myself, would make up for any lack of experience.

How wrong I was! They all stayed on an extra couple of hours that evening. I acted as facilitator, which in hindsight was a facile decision. We filled a flipchart with all the reasons why we could not cut the cost estimate, and then another on why the schedule was already far too short. We found a load more problems and risks that no one had thought of before. Then, of course, we became irritable and began criticising one another. In the end we had to adjourn the session, agreeing to try again later in the week. The whole episode had been a waste of time. I went home feeling thoroughly dejected.

When Larry got back I told him all about the futile brainstorming session.

"Do you think it was a good idea to hold the session after a long day's work?" he asked.

"There was a diary problem. It was the only time we could all manage," I told him.

Larry shook his head. "One of the most important ingredients of success in opportunity planning is the alertness and enthusiasm of the team," he said. "Tired people can't be expected to produce good plans, you know."

Tired people rarely make good plans

"OK. But you could say that of any kind of work," I replied. "Tired people make more mistakes. Isn't that what you're getting at?"

It wasn't. Larry told me that making mistakes is not an issue in opportunity planning. He said the very idea of making a mistake is alien to the imaginative processes necessary for opportunity management. Tiredness, on the other hand, *is* a problem because it can suppress creativity. Tired children often say they are bored, when what they really mean is they don't find playing exciting any more. Adults also need to be alert if they are to be at their most creative, and that means not overworked.

Tired thinkers are unlikely to have original thoughts

Larry suggested that if you find creative thinking hard work you may simply be too tired and, as a result, trying too hard. A little bit of unconventional thinking goes a long way towards creating new ideas.

Creativity isn't about thinking hard; it's about thinking unconventionally

"But there's so much to do," I told him. "Our department is a lot smaller than it used to be. We have to work on into the evening most days just to keep our heads above water."

Larry shrugged. "Maybe you're right," he said. "But you ought to be aware of the consequences. I saw an interesting survey the other day. It said that 95 per cent of managers do at least one hour of overtime a day and getting on for half of them do an average of three extra hours. That's equivalent to two extra working days per week. Your people deserve the opportunity to be creative. But how can they ever be truly imaginative in their work if you keep pushing them as much as you are now? They won't. That's my opinion."

"So what do I do? Ban all overtime?" I snapped.

Larry did not rise to the bait. He told me that overtime might well be necessary occasionally, but it isn't a cure-all. He said there are times when a team can only function effectively if they are *not* under the pressure of an imminent deadline – if they can make mistakes without others getting angry and accusing them of letting the side down. He said creative thinking is only successful when stretching the imagination is perceived as exciting and non-threatening. For many people error terror – the fear of making mistakes, of being ridiculed – is a barrier to creativity.

Creative thinking flourishes in a non-threatening environment, free from the fear of failure and the risk of ridicule

I asked Larry if he had any ideas for avoiding error terror when preparing opportunity-management plans.

"Here's one," he replied. "Make sure that everyone in the planning session does plenty of laughing before you try to focus their creativity. For example, if you are leading the group, *you* should be the first to do something silly. Give them a reason to laugh at *you*."

"You mean like wearing a funny hat and a false nose?" I asked.

"Why not? And get everyone else to do something outlandish, too."

"I really don't think my people would be at all happy with that suggestion," I told him. "Don't get me wrong, they're a good team. But frankly they're rather a serious bunch. They think larking about is a waste of time. To be honest, so do I."

"All right, Jim. Give them the morning off. Then show a Tom and Jerry cartoon or something before you start your opportunity-planning session. Oh – and do wear the funny hat. At *least* do that."

"You're joking!"

"Never been more serious in my life," he insisted.

"Oh yes? And suppose the chief exec bursts in on our meeting. What then?"

"Give *him* a funny hat. Get him to join in."

"You can't be serious," I said. Larry didn't say a word, but I could see that he was deadly serious.

"Anyway why waste the morning session?" I added.

"I'll tell you why," he said. "What time do your people start work in the mornings? Nine o'clock?" I nodded, and he continued, "Then break the routine. Dress casually. Meet at the beach or in a park. Not in your office or some stuffy old conference room. When you need extraordinary results, make everything else extraordinary. There's not much chance of finding a unicorn in a conference room."

When you need extraordinary results, create an extraordinary situation

It made sense. I had been driving my tired troops into battle with little concern for preparation and no thought of what equipment they might need. After working flat out on the Bilston plan for six weeks, they deserved a break. I wasn't convinced of the wisdom of discussing commercially sensitive information on the beach or in a park, but the principle of getting away from our traditional surroundings had to be right. There were plenty of other venues where we could enjoy new surroundings and still retain the security we needed. On the other hand, who in their right mind would take any notice of the rantings of a group of scruffy people wearing funny hats and false noses and cavorting about on the beach? There was probably a much higher chance of a conference venue being bugged than of our discussion on the beach being overheard and taken seriously.

"Ordinary people can produce quite extraordinary results if only they can shake off traditional thinking and stop being reasonable," Larry said.

Ordinary people can produce extraordinary ideas when they stop analysing and start being unreasonable

"But you have got to equip your team properly," he added.

"How do I do that?" I asked.

"It's not difficult," he assured me. "All you need to do is to maintain the right environment – a creative, no-risk atmosphere – and ensure that they use imaginative processes rather than analytical ones. A critical, negative atmosphere is the enemy of creativity."

"I see. So the first thing I have to do is to create a positive atmosphere. How do I do that?"

"Be positive yourself. Encourage and praise those who contribute ideas. Show that saying unreasonable things is not just acceptable but is really valued. Don't criticise half-baked suggestions. Accept conflicting views. And don't keep looking at your watch – no time pressures, remember!"

"I'll try," I told him. "But it's all so very different from the rest of the work."

"Different from the rest of *your* work, perhaps. But if you were in Advertising, or any of dozens of other jobs where creativity is highly valued, you would find these suggestions perfectly acceptable if not the norm."

"OK," I conceded. "And what about your second point – ensuring that the team uses imaginative processes rather than analytical ones? Talk me through that, please."

Larry said that analytical processes are based upon logical, step-by-step reasoning. He gave as an example the process of finding and fixing a fault on a motorbike. The motorbike is travelling up a hill when suddenly the engine stops pulling and the bike slows to a halt.

"Would you assume that the engine needs a few more pistons?" he asked. I shook my head. "No, of course not," he continued. "It can't be that, because the bike used to be OK. You would run through various reasons why the engine might stop pulling. Out of fuel? Fuel pipe blocked? Alternator failure? Loose electrical connection? The list is huge. But a few simple questions would eliminate most of these."

I couldn't fault his logic, but equally I couldn't see where it was leading.

"Is the engine still running?" he continued. "Let's say it is. All right, then is the bike still set in gear? No? Then maybe that last gear change wasn't made properly. Is the gear lever in neutral? Yes? Right, depress the clutch and try selecting first gear. OK now? Good! And a lot easier than redesigning the engine."

All this was basic common sense to me, and I said so.

"Let's not get into a discussion on the endangered species known as common sense," Larry replied. "Most problem-solving processes rely on logic and experience. Something was all right in the past and now it is not, and you need to put it back the way it was. Repairing things, finding something that you have lost – these sorts of problems can be solved by restoring some past condition. But there are other types of problems that can only be solved by finding entirely new solutions. A walk down Memory Lane won't help you with these. You need to create something that has never existed before, and for this you require imaginative ideas. You need to use quite different thought processes. Imagination, creativity, innovation. The really significant leaps forward are usually based on nonsense, not on common sense."

Great leaps forward are usually based more on nonsense than on common sense

"Incremental evolution," Larry continued, "is an interminable series of tiny steps made with one foot always on firm soil, known territory. But revolutionary change – the great leap forward that puts you way ahead of the opposition – comes from irrational, illogical thought. If it makes sense it probably isn't innovative and it almost certainly won't be revolutionary. The obvious has been thoroughly searched for opportunities already."

Ideas that make immediate sense are the least likely to lead to major innovations

"I think I see what you are getting at," I said. "But how do I get my team to think creatively? How do *you* do it, Larry? Give me a clue!"

"OK! But before my team and I try to think up creative solutions to a problem, we always have a warm-up exercise, just to get our brains out of the logical ruts they have to run in most of the time. Last week, for example, I asked them to organise a brainstorming session to come up with ideas for crossing a wide, deep river. The assumption was that we had arrived at the river, miles from anywhere, only to discover that the bridge had been swept away in a flood. Here are the ideas they came up with."

Larry rummaged through his filing cabinet and fished out a sheet of flipchart paper.

√ Swim across   √ Dam the river   √ Dig a tunnel

√ Fly by plane   √ Use a different upstream

                                        √ Go to another bridge

        √ Make a boat

                              X Walk under water on the river bed

                    √ Stepping stones

X Pole vault

                                    X Drain off the water

        √ Rebuild the bridge

                              X Human catapult

    X Freeze the water and walk across

X Walk on water   X Make river narrow enough to step across

Some of the suggestions had ticks against them. The stupid ones, I noticed, had crosses.

"Oh, I get it," I said. "You brainstorm a whole lot of ideas without worrying whether they are good or bad, and then you sort them out afterwards."

"That's right," Larry said.

"And that's why the useless suggestions have crosses – right?" I asked.

Myth
When you have eliminated the impossible, what remains is the right answer

"No, not really," Larry replied. "Those with ticks against them are the ones we *know* can work – and if our competitors were holding a brainstorming session right now you can bet those ideas would be on their list, too. Sadly, all too often brainstorm sessions produce nothing more than a list of ideas people have seen or heard about before. They are little more than exercises in memory recall."

Many brainstorm sessions are nothing more than a walk down Memory Lane

I had to admit that Larry had very neatly summed up our own attempts at brainstorming.

"But this brainstorm brought out some really creative thinking," Larry went on. "And those aren't crosses beside the zany ideas, by the way. They are kisses. We love 'em. They are the ideas that seem to make no sense. When we're looking for a breakthrough, it is only the nonsensical ideas that we bother to investigate in more detail. If we were to analyse the suggestions for the things we *know* could be made to work, we would almost certainly come back to rebuilding the original bridge. And so would anyone else who is familiar with the world as we know it today."

When you have eliminated what is currently possible, what remains includes the future

"And you'll notice that most of the zany ideas came out towards the end of the brainstorming session. That's quite normal. It's why we always try to go through what we call the unsound barrier. That usually means getting more than a dozen ideas."

When brainstorming for novel ideas, try to go through the 'unsound barrier'

"Look," Larry said as he turned the page of his flipchart. "Here is the tidy copy of our brainstorm, ready for more detailed analysis."

> X Walk under the river bed
> X Pole vault
> X Drain off the water
> X Human catapult
> X Freeze water and walk across
> X Make river narrow enough to step across
> X Walk on water

I was beginning to think that Larry was having me on.

"How is this going to help?" I asked.

"Currently," he said, "we're working on this idea for an ice bridge for use on rivers in remote areas prone to flooding. Basically we fit light-weight wooden shuttering across the river, install a refrigeration grid and run the compressors. Then we throw water at it. In a few hours the ice is thick enough to carry trucks, trains, anything you want. Ice is amazingly tough stuff, you know, and it has the advantage that the raw materials are always available on site. If the river floods, the ice bridge simply floats upwards, returning to its normal position once the water subsides. Of course, we do have to keep the whole thing frozen. The cooling system is backed up by solar cells, and so it is at its most efficient in hot weather when it is most needed. Resurfacing the bridge is simplicity itself – pour on more water, run the cooling system flat out for half an hour, and then cover the surface with a layer of gravel from the river bed. Even if our bridge *is* destroyed in a massive flood we can rebuild it for a fraction of the cost of a conventional one."

"Wow! That's fantastic," I said.

"Yes, I'm afraid it is," Larry replied with a grin. "Pure fantasy. But if it *had* worked we would have made a real breakthrough. Anyway, I hope this has convinced you of the tremendous potential of irrational thinking."

It had shown just how easily I could be taken in by Larry Farlow. But again he had made his point. Ice on a road bridge, which is usually considered a problem, can be turned on its head – a road bridge on ice – to create an opportunity. And eliminating the logical approaches, the sensible ideas, the obviously feasible suggestions from the output of a brainstorm session can be a way of creating a list of irrational ideas that might lead to a breakthrough.

This was interesting. And simple. And you didn't have to be a genius to understand the process. If I could get my team to think this way it had to be possible to find, or maybe even to create, opportunities to help us with the Bilston job. *If* we could get our minds to work in the right way.

I wanted to give it a go while Larry was there to help me.

"OK then, Larry," I said. "Try this. If a hole in a balloon is a problem, how about a balloon in a hole as an idea for finding an opportunity?"

"And how does that help?" he challenged.

"I don't know – yet," I replied. "But when I do I'm sure it will be useful for something – hey! Wait a minute, don't they use that kind of thing to help people with furred-up arteries – pushing a tiny balloon along the artery and then pumping it up?"

"Exactly!" Larry agreed. "And if you had thought of that idea a few years ago we wouldn't now be discussing whether a balloon in a hole is a silly idea. Never throw away any of the so-called *silly* ideas that come out of truly imaginative brainstorm-ing sessions. They often come in useful when you're working on something completely unrelated to the subject of the session that produced them. But of course, there are lots of other ways of launching a creative idea-generation session."

"Such as?" I asked.

"Well, how about listing things that have not the slightest connection with what it is you are hoping to achieve. Here – I'll show you."

Larry delved into his filing cabinet again and brought out another flipchart page. "The subject of this creativity session was 'Ideas for Improving Customer Care'," he said. "Can you see any links between the things written here and the subject of the session?"

Ideas for Improving Customer Care

Chess　　　**Mowing the lawn**

　　　　　　　　　　　Pale blue poppies

Snails in a sandstorm

　　　　　　　　Midnight in Moscow

　　　Polar bear Pate

　　　　　　　　　Concertinas

Dead leaves

　　　　　　　　　　Photography

　　　Background noise

"None whatsoever," I said. "At least the ideas on the first brainstorm list were *attempts* at solving the problem. This lot appears to be completely useless. To me this really *is* nonsense, Larry."

"OK. But now let's search for links between these things listed here and improving customer care. Take dead leaves, for example. What can you say about them?"

"Nothing that's likely to be of any use," I replied.

"How do you know until you try? Don't be so negative. What about – they're dead, but if we use them as compost they could bring life to other plants?"

"That's true, but I still don't see how . . ."

"All right. Now what about past customers who have retired from business? Could we find a way of getting some of them to help nurture our budding relationships with new customers?"

"I don't know," I said. "I suppose many of them will still be in touch with their profession, whatever that was. And possibly even with the organisation they worked for. Maybe that could help in some way – *if only* we could find out which people had retired from which organisation."

"Good!" Larry said. "And we can tell what sort of tree a dead leaf came from, can't we?"

"Well, yes," I agreed. "There are always clues – size, shape, the pattern of the veins – I'm no expert, but there are people who know about these things."

"And in the same way," Larry said, "there might be links which still bond past customers to their parent organisations and professions. Worth investigating further?"

"Yes, I'd say so," I replied. "And you're suggesting that every one of the ideas on this chart could be developed in the same way?"

"That's right. It's not the suggestion itself that matters but what you make of it. The things it prompts you to consider."

The biggest opportunities often start life as tiny, unintelligible things, as do all babies

"Some people call this *springboarding*," he continued, "because your creativity rises to greater heights using the initial idea as a launch platform."

Only with the nourishment of rotten ideas can good ideas take root

"And then what do we do?" I asked.

"Well, the very last thing we do is to analyse all the material that a creative session has produced. But we never do the analysis straight after the creative bit. *Never!*"

"OK, Larry. I suppose I'll have to ask the dumb question. Why not?"

"Because every one of these ideas is somebody's brainchild, and it's not a clever move to ridicule someone's new-born baby. Rejoice in the birth. Let them cuddle their creation a while. Let it grow up. We all know that nobody is perfect, not even our own children. The time for criticism is definitely not immediately after the birth."

Only a fool would ridicule a new-born baby – especially someone else's brainchild

"In any case," Larry continued, "we are always on a high at the end of one of our creative sessions. We need to calm down before we can be objective in assessing the pros and cons of the various options. But, of course, we do need to reduce our options to a shortlist before doing a more detailed analysis."

Imagination produces; logic deduces; rationalisation reduces

"So when *do* you do the analysis?" I asked.

"A day or so later, if that's at all possible. By that time we are more likely to be constructively critical of our own suggestions as well as other people's. We have a whole range of analytical tools and techniques to check the feasibility, viability and so on. Technical compliance, cost–benefit analysis, cash flow, return on investment, profit forecasts, risk analysis. All the usual stuff. We need to be serious, thorough and objective at this stage. Quite unlike the creative thinking processes that produced the ideas in the first place."

Larry looked at me as if expecting to find a converted soul ready to carry the banner. But although I couldn't fault his logic I still felt uneasy.

"All it suggests to me," I said, "is that it is totally unreasonable to ask people to concentrate on managing risks and analysing options, and at the same time to expect them to recognise, to search for and to create opportunities."

"I agree," Larry replied. "The atmosphere in which each of these processes can flourish is so different. That's why we keep a risk register and an opportunity log – but we don't try to deal with the two together. We need mainly analytical processes for assessing our risk management but a lot more creative thinking when reviewing opportunity management."

Creativity thrives in an environment where imagination can run wild

"Right," I said. "I follow all that. But we can't choose what we do. Bilstons decide that. How can we find opportunities when what we have got to do is pretty much set in concrete? Help me, Larry. I need something that will convince Jean Cartwright."

Larry wriggled uncomfortably, and I waded in with another salvo: "And there's the far-from-insignificant matter of selling the idea to a team of hardened sceptics. These guys have been through a tough time, lately. They're not used to hearing good news. How do I convince *them*? And maybe I still need to convince myself."

All I got from Larry was a sympathetic smile. I broke the uneasy silence.

"I don't want to sound negative," I said, "but it's all very theoretical. I need something real. Haven't you got any real-world examples that I could show to my team? They're all practical people. They find new ideas easier to grasp when they can see applications for them in the world of work."

Larry had been expecting that one.

"Probably the most convincing arguments come from turning risk into opportunity," he said. "If you could show them that there are real opportunities masquerading as risks in the Bilston contract, that ought to clinch it."

"Agreed!" I said. "And how do I do that?"

"Dunno," he replied with a nonchalant shrug. "That's *your* job. You and your team."

"Thanks a heap!" I said. "Just when we get to the point where you really could help us you say it's up to me and my team to sort it. Haven't you got *anything* to offer? Not even an example or two that we could copy? We need something to build on."

"There are plenty of examples, all around you. There are people turning risk and failure into opportunity and success every day. They're not all spectacular achievements, but they add up to a great deal."

Then Larry told me about one of Sir Clive Sinclair's early initiatives. As an entrepreneur, Sinclair is probably best remembered for making the affordable home computer a reality. Had he followed the traditional route of incorporating disk drives and a conventional keyboard, his ZX81 and Spectrum computers would have been beyond the means of most people; but he used a humble audio cassette recorder and a very basic membrane keypad.

But before becoming the father of the home-computer industry, Clive Sinclair saw and exploited the opportunity for pocket calculators. And way back in the 1960s, before the birth of the pocket calculator, he developed a very successful business buying and selling faulty semiconductor transistors.

Who in his right mind would purposely buy faulty electronic components?

In the early days of semiconductor manufacture, the risk of whole batches of transistors being well below specification, or even not functioning at all, was extremely high. Then, as now, it was virtually impossible to repair a faulty semiconductor device. Yields of good devices were low, and scrap rates were high and unpredictable. Naturally most people would have considered faulty transistors to be useless junk. To the manufacturers they had very little scrap value, and so Sinclair was able to buy them up cheaply. He then sorted them according to the degree of life they exhibited. Even a transistor with no amplification capability whatsoever could often be used as a diode, a much simpler two-terminal device requiring only one junction of the transistor to be intact. Amateur enthusiasts, not always needing the ultimate in performance from an electronic component, clamoured for Sinclair's transistors and diodes at prices they could afford.

"One person's risk of failure can present a golden opportunity for another," Larry concluded.

One person's risk can be another person's golden opportunity

"That's all very well," I said, "but we're not all as entrepreneurial as Clive Sinclair. And most people never will be. Some of us have to keep the business running smoothly. Business-as-usual work isn't free from risks, you know. How can your ideas help people in ordinary jobs?"

Far from being fazed by my outburst, Larry seemed quite pleased.

"Good point," he said. "Opportunity management is for everyone – any work that contains risks is potentially a source of opportunity."

"If only *we* were living in the golden age of opportunity," I said.

Larry grinned. "We are, Jim," he said, and he handed me a battered old file that might once have been a personal organiser. It was labelled 'Opportunities: Larry Farlow', and its pages were of thick card rather than ordinary paper.

"Whenever I have an idea that I think might lead to an opportunity, I jot it down as a heading on a fresh page," he said. "Then I keep adding details to the ideas as they occur to me. I note any links with other opportunities – new or better ways of doing things, and so on – and gradually the whole picture becomes clearer."

"I think I follow the gist," I said, thumbing through the book. "But what about these here? They're all marked with crosses. Are they the ideas that turned out to be no good?"

Larry rolled his eyes and let out a long sigh.

"You still don't understand even the most basic principle of opportunity management, do you? There is no such thing as a useless idea. The ones with crosses, as you call them – and once again, Jim, they're kisses – they are the ones that have proved useful already. They are already stars, if you like."

There is no such thing as a useless original idea

"Oh, I see. Then why haven't you taken them out of the binder once they have been used?" I asked, without thinking it through.

Larry looked at me as if I were brain-dead. He spoke very slowly.

"There's nothing to be ashamed of in copying good ideas," he said. "Especially your own. You'll notice there is a 'Copycat' section near the front of the binder. All the ideas in that section have at least one star. That's because after I have found an opportunity and made use of it I *know* that it's worth copying *and* I know how to exploit it. That makes it doubly valuable. So I move it into the 'Copycat' section, which is the first place I look when I need creative ideas for solving a new problem. That's one of the reasons I prefer to use a ring binder: so that I can move ideas about easily."

There's nothing to be ashamed of in copying good ideas – especially your own

Larry turned the pages until he came to what he was looking for. "Look here – this one has got four kisses. It's a four-star idea. This particular idea has helped me in four different situations so far. In the 'New Ideas' section I keep any ideas that haven't proven useful yet. They haven't yet earned their stars, but that's almost certainly due more to my limitations rather than to any fault of their own."

The way he spoke, it all sounded very straightforward. But managing opportunity couldn't be that simple, or everyone would be doing it. I asked him why he kept his opportunity log to himself rather than having a file that everyone in the team could share. He had an answer, of course. He explained that, like many people, he had to work on more than one job at a time – he was a part-time member of several teams. For each job the team needs to keep a combined risk register and opportunity log. This is a sort of database (although most people are likely to make more use of a hard copy, with a page for each risk and the facing page for any related opportunities). Most important of all, this information is available at all times to *all* team members.

"But I still keep my personal opportunity notebook, of course," Larry added.

"I see, so is it in the group log that you cross off opportunities once you have exploited them?" I asked.

"I suppose you *could* do," he replied, "but in my team we prefer not to, for two reasons. First, with a little more creative thinking it's often possible to increase the benefits from an opportunity – or perhaps to find benefits for a customer or for one of our key suppliers. And second, every success in opportunity management fuels the motivation of the team. So we prefer to leave our achievements on display. They remind us how worthwhile our creative sessions have been."

It sounded convincing enough and prompted me to ask: "When you are updating your risk register, wouldn't it be a good idea to strike through any risk that has been averted rather than removing the page completely?"

Hiding successes
is as unhelpful as
hiding problems

"Yes, I think you're right," Larry said. "A resolved risk can sometimes re-emerge, of course. But in any case, keeping achievements on display is part of sharing among the whole team anything we learn individually. This is as important as celebrating individual successes as team triumphs and not just as personal ones. Maintaining team spirit on long-term, difficult jobs is never easy, and these are two really important sources of motivation. Nobody can afford to waste these kinds of opportunities."

"Could I borrow your opportunity notebook – just for a day or so?" I asked.

Larry gave me a withering look.

"I'll bring it back," I said. "I promise."

"Look at the state of your desk, Jim," he said. "A whole library could get lost for years among all that bumph."

He stared at me coolly for a few seconds.

"Sorry. The answer's still no," he said. "But what I can let you have – to keep, if you like – are copies of a few pages from one of our risk registers, complete with their opportunity log entries."

I waited while Larry organised the photocopying, and then I got myself a coffee and sat down to do some serious thinking about what he had been telling me. I summarised the key points in my opportunity notebook.

Subject: Making an opportunity management plan

- Tired people rarely make the most imaginative plans.
- Creativity isn't about thinking hard; it's about thinking unconventionally.
- Creative thinking flourishes in a non-threatening environment, free from the fear of failure and the risk of ridicule.
- Ordinary people can produce extraordinary results when they stop analysing and start being unreasonable.
- Ideas that make immediate sense are the least likely to be innovative; it is unwise, therefore, to discard nonsensical suggestions.
- When you have eliminated what is currently possible, that which remains includes the future.
- The biggest opportunities often start life as tiny, unintelligible things, as do all babies.
- Good ideas can take root and grow more rapidly if fed with the nourishment of rotten ideas.
- Don't ridicule someone else's brainchild; it might hold the key to your future success.
- Imagination produces; logic deduces; rationalisation reduces.
- Creativity thrives in an environment where Imagination can run wild.
- One man's risk can be another man's golden opportunity.
- There is no such thing as a useless original idea.
- Hiding successes is as unhelpful as hiding problems.

Action: I must learn how to make *and use* an opportunity-management plan.

Chapter 6

Beauty and the beast:
finding opportunity within risk

In what seemed no time at all, the two months Bilstons had given us to prepare our bid had almost vanished. Now we had just five days before Jean's review meeting – seven if you were to include the weekend. But I couldn't: Mary was counting on us visiting her parents. It was their Golden Wedding anniversary, and if I couldn't even find time for that – No, the weekend was spoken for. Five days, then, to find cost savings of 15 per cent and to convince Jean and ourselves that we could meet the Bilston schedule.

I spent a couple of hours with Jill and Pete, checking the commercial section of the proposal. Then I called in on the Customer Support team – fortunately they had created no new problems for me – and I headed for home. I needed the quiet of my study to concentrate on some important homework.

In the car park I almost collided with Jean Cartwright. She was coming in!

"Off early, Jim? Can I take it you've no problem in cutting the estimate by 15 per cent?"

"Nothing that staying any later would alter," I told her. Then curiosity got the better of me.

"What brings you back in?" I asked

"The old man's called an evening meeting. All the divisional directors and a couple of other people. See you tomorrow."

Well, well – Jean Cartwright working late, I thought. It must be something very dear to old Gilbert's heart, too. It's not like the old man to burn the midnight oil. Breakfast meetings are more his style – I had been to a couple of those. (7 a.m. is not one of my best times of day, but the chief exec's office is always buzzing by that time.)

I wished her goodnight and set off home. On the way my thoughts switched back to my earlier encounter, with Larry Farlow. If Larry had been suffering from fatigue after his long journey he had hidden it very well. Or maybe he had somehow transferred his tiredness to me, because my mind was still struggling way back on the trail of the unicorn.

The file I borrowed from Larry contained a combined risk register and opportunity log for designing and building a transport depot for an intercontinental haulage contractor. Transport division had completed the construction work and got the new depot up and running well within the planned eighteen-month schedule.

Guidance notes at the beginning of each section of the risk register made the job of sorting out what it all meant a whole lot easier. Right at the front of the register was a description of two types of risks – global risks and specific risks.

Global risks are those common to most jobs, and not specifically related to the work involved. An example would be the risk of losing key people. The result of staff losses is delay and extra expense, especially if you have to recruit or train replacement specialists. And if you cannot get suitable replacements, you might be unable to complete the job at all, with all the financial and credibility loss that would entail. Other global risks include economic recession, a major epidemic of influenza, a hostile takeover bid, and so on. Global risks can sometimes be offset by global opportunities – opportunities that are available to everyone. The risk of losing key people could be offset by seizing the opportunity to train and develop others, thereby increasing the capability of the individuals, their teams and the business itself. Often, if you go about it in the right way, these benefits can more than offset the cost of the training.

Other global opportunities might include developing partnerships to increase business capability and to obtain the benefits of increased synergy – where the capability of the partnership is much greater than the sum of the capabilities of the constituent parts.

The first section of the register was an assessment of the degree of global risk in the job. It had been prepared three months before the customer had even begun talking about the possibility of a contract. Entries were in the form of a checklist. This was very similar to my own approach except that in each case, rather than simply stating the risk area, the nature of the risk was briefly described:

Nature of risk:
- The customer's budget might change or disappear
- The required timescale might be unreasonably short
- Our best price might exceed the customer's budget
- Success might depend critically on factors outside our control
- New technologies used might not be mature and stable
- Key subcontractors might not have the necessary resources available
- Market needs might change, leading to contract cancellation
- Requirements might not be fully understood at contract date
- Requirements might change significantly during contract
- We might not have the necessary resources to develop the system
- We might not have the necessary resources to support the system

Overall exposure to risk:
- Risk of market upheaval and other commercial problems   L
- Risk of technical non-compliance   M
- Risk of schedule slippage   H

General approach to be taken:
- Investigate rapid-development options as this could be critically important to our winning the contract
- Maintain close links with the customer to ensure that the expectations and the budget remain compatible
- Look for opportunities to gain experience of the new technology on existing work within the division or farther afield

---

Interesting though all this was, it didn't take me any nearer to finding the time and cost savings I needed on the Bilston job. The next section looked more hopeful, however: it was about job-specific risks and opportunities and there was a lot more detail to it. Although very different from my usual approach, it appeared to be the sort of thing we needed to do, so I took a look at some of the work-specific risks and their corresponding opportunity logs.

In Larry's system, each risk is on a separate page and in a standard format (although in this instance some sections were left blank). All entries are dated and, rather than amending entries as work advances and more becomes known about the risks, any changes are given a new page. The advantage is that you can see at a glance what has changed between the latest entry and all previous ones. Ultimately, you build up a historic record of the perceived risk and how it was managed.

Here is a typical entry compiled at a time when Larry was preparing a rough-order-of-magnitude cost indication for this potential customer:

Risk Register ref: *R12*	Version: *1* Date: *7/8/1996*
Owner	*L Farlow*
Description of risk	*The new facility might suffer from excessive queueing times, and this problem might only become apparent during proving trials. This would not be acceptable to the customer and so we would have to make significant changes to resolve the problem*
Cost, schedule, performance, credibility loss if the risk is realised (High/Medium/Low, or quantified where possible)	*M delay to completion* *L cost of late changes to software*
Customer's perception that this risk is serious (H,M,L)	*H – customer is very concerned at any threat to completion target*
Probability of the risk being realised: (H,M,L or P%)	*M*
Risk exposure – the cost of doing nothing or correcting the problem reactively multiplied by the probability of occurrence	*Schedule risk exposure is M × M, but because of customer's concerns we need to be seen to take this matter very seriously*
Proactive counter-measures to reduce impact/probability	*Unknown*
Cost and time required for proactive counter-measures (to be included in baseline plan for the job)	*Unknown*
Residual risk after proactive counter-measures (description)	*Unknown*
Impact of residual risk (additional cost, delay, etc. – H/M/L, or quantified if possible)	*Unknown*
Probability of residual risk being realised (H,M,L or P%)	*Unknown*
Contingency plan for dealing reactively with residual risk	*None known at this stage*
Cost and timescale for fallback plan	*Unclear*
Management reserve for fallback plan (Contingency plan cost × P%)	*Unclear*
Any new risks introduced by this mitigation plan (describe, quantify and create new risk register entry if necessary)	*Unknown*

At this stage the only thing recorded was that excessive queueing times could be a problem and sorting it out might delay completion of the job and cost a relatively small amount of money. This was not viewed by the experts in the company as a particularly serious risk; however, Amsys wanted to be seen to be taking it seriously because it was of great concern to the customer, who felt that anything that might delay completion deserved special attention. There was no analysis other than the general assessment that the risk was moderately high, its impact on the cost of the job would not be very great, but the effect on the schedule might be significant. Nothing was recorded about how the risk might be managed.

The facing page was the corresponding opportunity log. It was even more skeletal than the risk register entry. There was some vague reference to the kinds of opportunities that might be found or created and the sorts of benefits they might provide, but no specific opportunities had been identified. It was all extremely hazy.

Opportunity Log reference: 012	Version: 1 Date: 7/8/1996
Owner	L Farlow
Description of opportunities sought/ expected	If we can reduce the risk of excessive queueing on this new facility, we might be able to fine-tune other existing installations to improve their performance at peak-load times.
Who would benefit?	Our customers and potential customers for new installations. (This could be a useful service that we could sell profitably.)
Expected or targeted magnitude of benefits	Undefined
– Achieved to date:	Nil
– Remaining target to meet and beat:	Undefined
Copycat opportunities (whom can we copy; what could we copy?)	Unknown
– Found and exploited to date:	None
– Planned actions with dates:	To be decided
Windfall opportunities (where should we be; when should we be there?)	Unknown
– Found and exploited to date:	None
– Planned actions with dates:	None
Hidden opportunities (how can the unexpected be turned to advantage?)	Unknown
– Revealed and exploited to date:	None
– Planned actions with dates:	To be decided
Imagineered opportunities (what processes could we use, and when?)	Unknown
– Created and exploited to date:	None
– Planned actions with dates:	To be decided

Turning the page I found a later version, completed at a time when a formal proposal and a fixed-price quotation were being prepared. Not only had the nature and likely magnitude of the risk been investigated in more detail, but there was also an outline plan of how the risk might be managed.

Once again, the facing page was the opportunity log. But now, some three months on, the team had some idea of what they were looking for in the way of opportunities. They wanted to cut twenty minutes off the queueing time at peak periods and to improve the average turn-round time by ten minutes. They also needed to gather independent evidence for these performance claims so that they could market the service more widely.

The opportunity log contained a few ideas of where and when to look for windfalls: an opportunity-management plan was beginning to take shape, although it didn't contain anything like enough guidance to be useful to me and my team. I just hoped the whole process would become a lot clearer once we got round to planning our own work.

Risk Register reference: *R12*	Version: *2* Date: *2/11/1996*
Owner	*L Farlow*
Description of risk	*The new facility might suffer from excessive queueing times during peak loads, particularly during wet weather when loading takes longer than normal.*
Cost, schedule, performance, credibility loss if the risk is realised (High/ Medium/Low, or quantified where possible)	*Estimated addition cost of £6000 and 9 weeks' delay to completion.*
Customer's perception that this risk is serious (H,M,L)	*H*
Probability of the risk being realised: (H,M,L or P%)	*20%*
Risk exposure − the cost of doing nothing or correcting the problem reactively multiplied by the probability of occurrence	*£1200 and 1.8 weeks' delay, but because of customer's concerns we need to be seen to take the matter of schedule risk very seriously.*
Proactive measures to reduce impact and/or probability of risk	*Computer modelling and optimisation prior to installation.*
Cost and time required for proactive risk mitigation (to be included in baseline budget for the job)	*£3000; no extension of overall programme.*
Residual risk (description of risk remaining despite mitigation measures)	*Some fine tuning might still be necessary due to modelling inaccuracies.*
Impact of residual risk (additional cost, delay, etc. − High/Medium/Low, or quantified if possible)	*£800; no schedule implications.*
Probability of residual risk being realised (High, Medium, Low or %)	*10%*
Contingency plan for dealing reactively with residual risk	*Fine-tune system during the first quarter of the warranty period*
Residual risk management reserve (contingency plan cost and timescale x% probability)	*£80; no schedule implications*
Any new risks introduced by this mitigation plan (describe, quantify, and create new risk register entry if necessary)	*None*

Opportunity Log reference: 012	Version: 2 Date: 21/11/1996
Owner	L Farlow
Description of opportunities sought/ expected	If we can reduce the risk of excessive queueing on this new facility, we might be able to fine-tune other existing installations to improve their performance at peak load times.
Who would benefit?	Our customers and potential customers for new installations. (This could be a useful service that we could sell profitably.)
Expected or targeted magnitude of benefits	Reduce peak queueing time by 20 min. Reduce average turn-round time by 10 min.
– Achieved to date:	Nil
– Remaining target to meet and beat:	As above
Copycat opportunities (whom can we copy; what could we copy?)	Unknown
– Found and exploited to date:	None
– Planned actions with dates:	LF to survey all Amsys divisions by 1/2/97. PJK to consult RW/AME and report by 19/1/97
Windfall opportunities (where should we be; when should we be there?)	Unknown
– Found and exploited to date:	None
– Planned actions with dates:	PJK to visit SimulEx conference 2–4/2/97 and contact organisations with similar needs to our own
Hidden opportunities (how can the unexpected be turned to advantage?)	Unknown
– Revealed and exploited to date:	None
– Planned actions with dates:	To be decided
Imagineered opportunities (what processes could we use, and when?)	Unknown
– Created and exploited to date:	None
– Planned actions with dates:	To be decided

After lunch on Thursday, I got together with the team and we had another look at our own plan. This time, we tried to identify the actual risks. We found twenty-three significant ones – we were quite good at looking on the black side. The next step was to position them on the risk map, and taking Larry's advice we restricted attention to the top ten.

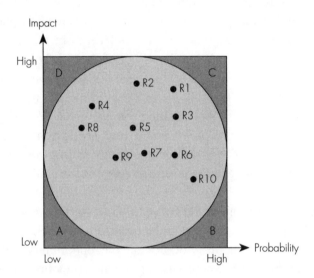

Our biggest concern was with the risk of the transmitter overheating. None of our previous installations had been subject to such wide climatic variations as were encountered at Delvington. We were particularly concerned about the cooling system, which relied on a simple heat exchanger. If the transmitter got too hot the system was designed to cut to reduced power or to shut down altogether. It was even possible that the installation would fail to meet its contracted reliability target, and then we would have to make expensive modifications *and* suffer a disgruntled customer. We thought there was only a small chance of that happening, but if it did we would be in real trouble. And if we waited until the problem hit us – our traditional wait-and-see crisis-management strategy – we would have no option but to post an engineer on site, day and night, to nurse the thing while we built a superior cooling system. On the other hand, if we went for the higher-grade cooling system right from the start, we might not be able to meet the required delivery date. That would cost us the whole contract, and we really needed the work.

We argued about options for dealing with this risk for half an hour but came up with nothing that would keep us within budget and not delay the job excessively, so we decided to park the problem and look at some of the other risks. In many cases it wasn't difficult to work out the effect of the risk being realised – most were of medium or low impact, but some appeared to be real show stoppers, offering the prospect of months of delay and taking us well into loss making on the deal. For some of the most worrying risks we could find no proactive counter-measures, try as we would. It was obvious that we needed to do something to reduce our exposure to risk, but we could not agree what.

Thinking that it might be better to leave the risk register for a while, I suggested a day trip to the coast, a few beach games and then a couple of hours working on the opportunity log. The suggestion met with synchronised groaning. They just weren't in the mood, and it seemed pointless even to try to convince them otherwise.

"Have you flipped completely?" Pete asked. "You do realise that we're only two weeks away from the deadline for putting in our tender. I didn't work through most of last weekend just so we could all take a mid-week holiday, you know."

"I was trying to be constructive," I said. "Why don't we give it a go? Heaven knows we need some sort of opportunity-management plan. We'll never win the contract otherwise."

"I don't mean to be negative, Jim," Nadia said. "But what's the point if we can't even make a risk-management plan?"

"OK then," I said. "Let's leave the opportunity log for the time being. Thanks for contributing this afternoon. It has been a useful session, even if we didn't get quite as far as we had hoped. I'll get this lot typed up and copied to you all. Maybe a tidy version will prompt a few ideas. Don't get despondent. We are getting there, gradually."

"Sure. Only the hard part left to do," Pete quipped. Dave and Nadia sniggered, but I could see that Jill wasn't amused: she hated negative attitudes.

Pete was right, of course. Listing the risks was no great achievement. Without solutions, a list of problems is not a lot of help. But what more could I do?

"Can't you get us some help from somewhere?" Jill asked. "Someone who could show us how to work out risk-management strategies and the like?"

"Yes. Why not ask that Farlow chap?" Dave suggested. "Isn't he supposed to be something of an expert on these matters?"

I had hoped to be in a position to tell Larry that we had used his approach to risk planning and obtained some useful results. But this was no time to let Pride block the path of Progress, so I promised the team I would try to get Larry to help us.

My division would have to pay for Larry's time, so I had to let Jean know what was going on and get her blessing. In any case, if she *was* going to throw any more spanners into the works, it had better be while we still had time to sort out the mess. And with just four days to the review meeting with the chief executive, we had very little time to waste.

Slipping past her secretarial barricade, I poked my head around Jean's door.

"Spare a minute?"

She looked up but did not reply. A zombie's welcome couldn't have been cooler: she just shrugged.

"Does that mean yes?" I asked.

"Yes. Of course," she said, flatly.

Had she received some bad news at the evening meeting, I wondered? Had Amsys decided to cut its losses and to close Comms division? No, it couldn't be that. Gilbert Manning wouldn't have kept the rest of us in the dark for even a minute. So it had to be something personal.

"Are you feeling all right, Jean?" I asked.

"Yes. I'm fine. Let's get on with it."

"OK," I said. "If you're sure. I just wanted you to know how we're getting on with the bid, and to get your agreement on the way ahead."

"You will be ready for Gilbert's meeting on Friday week, won't you?" she said.

"We'll be ready," I told her. "I don't know how on earth we're going to finish everything in the time, but we will. We will." (The repetition was meant to add emphasis, but it sounded a trifle feeble to me, so I didn't risk an encore.)

I showed Jean our list of major risks and the chart we had used to help set priorities.

She gave the chart a cursory glance. "As far as I can see it's the right sort of thing," she said. "But there's nowhere near enough information. We've got to show Bilstons that we can finish the job on schedule despite the risks. They won't lose any sleep over the financial risk *we* are taking, so long as we don't go broke half-way through the job and leave them in the lurch. And they know we're big enough to be able to take whatever knocks we get from this job. But schedule risk is quite a different matter. That's very much their concern, as well as ours."

"Right," I agreed. "We intend to include something about timescales once we've finished our analysis. By the way, I'm hoping to get Larry to help me run a couple of workshops with the team on Monday. We'll be off site for the day. OK?"

"That's cutting things a bit fine, isn't it?" she said. "You haven't forgotten that I need all the figures by Wednesday lunch-time, have you?"

I said that we were all well aware of that.

Jean nodded and turned back to the spreadsheet she had been working on when I came in. That was all. I could go now. No *'Thanks, Jim.'* No *'Pass on my best wishes to the team.'* No *'Let me know if there's anything I can do to help.'* If I had been an entry in a cell of her spreadsheet, she couldn't have wiped me from memory more easily.

I left her door wide open. She likes it shut.

I found Larry in the library. He said he was researching; Jean Cartwright would have called it skiving.

"Hi, Larry! Guess what? I'm stuck. I need your help."

"You, too," he said, obscurely.

I raised my eyebrows and waited for an explanation.

"Nothing. Forget it," he said with a chuckle. (The chuckle said '*Please press for details.*')

"Me and who else?" I asked.

Larry closed his book.

"Your boss. Jean Cartwright."

"Jean? Have you been upsetting her?"

"We had an evening meeting yesterday, with Gilbert and most of the divisional directors. She collared me afterwards and asked whether I was doing everything I could to help you on the Bilston bid."

"What did you say?" I asked.

"Oh, just that you were ignoring all my ideas and ploughing on towards certain failure."

"But, Larry! That's not . . ."

"Kidding!" he said. "C'mon, let's go to my office and let these people study in peace and quiet."

I looked around. There was nobody else in the library. I told him so.

"I know," he replied. "What does that say about our organisation?"

"Everybody's busy with their day job?" I suggested.

"Everybody's *too* busy with their day job," he corrected. "To me it says that nobody is looking to see what's new. Nobody's looking for copycat opportunities."

"Maybe they do their research early in the mornings, or in the evening after work, or at weekends, perhaps," I suggested.

He asked whether the library was open at weekends. I said I didn't know. He asked what time it opened in the morning, and how late it remained open at the end of the day. I didn't answer. He said "Quite. I won't ask how often you use the library."

"Hang on Larry," I said, defensively. "I do take stuff home to read. Lots of people do, I'll bet."

Larry smiled.

"That's what last night's meeting was all about. The old man had had an analysis done of our library usage. Some weeks ago he told me he was concerned that as an organisation we were not sufficiently innovative. I told him that I thought the first step towards innovation is imitation."

The first step towards innovation is imitation

"He didn't ask me what I meant," Larry continued. "Instead he asked me to explain it to the divisional directors. That's what I was doing last night. That and a few other ideas. I ran a two-hour seminar."

"Blimey. No wonder Jean was looking punch drunk this morning. You mean you started with copycat opportunities and went through the whole spectrum?"

Larry nodded.

"It must have been pretty scary for you. How did it go?"

"Very well," he said. "Very well indeed, Jim. Thanks to you."

"*Me*? What did I do?"

"You critiqued all my rehearsals. That's what you did. I had to make quite a few changes as a result of all the questions you had been asking me. The divvies' questions weren't half as searching as yours. But then, they're not yet at the stage where they need to apply the principles to real work. It certainly focuses the mind."

I had been wondering why Larry had taken so much trouble to help me, particularly during my cynical, negative periods. In the past couple of weeks I must have taken every minute of his two-days-a-week allowance for process consultation work.

"Working with you on the Bilston bid was just the sort of opportunity I was looking for," he went on. "I needed such a windfall, and this one was far too good to miss. Do you mind?"

"Not in the slightest," I told him. I could see how his need to prepare and present a really impressive seminar could be helped along by doing a thorough job of coaching me, and the summary notes would have been useful to both of us.

Larry told me that the next step in Gilbert Manning's strategy for refocusing the divisional directors on innovation was a workshop session. It was to be based on a real-life case study. The chief had given Larry three months to prepare the necessary material.

"It won't be an evening session this time," Larry said. "They'll have to do some creative thinking. I want to use the Bilston contract as my case study. Are you happy with that, Jim?"

"A drains-up review of what went wrong?" I asked. "Or a 'how we won the war' documentary?"

"Well, you're going to win, aren't you?" he asked.

I nodded.

"Sure? If not, I had better get on and find myself another case study."

"We're going to win," I told him emphatically. "And you're going to help us.

"OK, then," he said with a broad grin. "It's a win–win. Coaching you, training me."

I told Larry I wanted him to spend some time working with me and my team on our risk-management plan and opportunity log. I explained how Jean was insisting on including all the figures in her submission to the chief executive and that she wanted to see hard evidence that we could meet the schedule target. I also told him that we had found it fairly easy to produce our risk list.

"Actual risks? Not just risk areas this time?" he asked.

"Actual risks," I confirmed.

"And how about the risk-management plan? I bet you didn't find that so easy," he said.

"How did you guess?"

"It never is," Larry told me. "Not when there are big risks involved."

He asked whether I had scheduled the session late in the day or early when everyone was fresh, and I told him I had got that right.

"Good. And did you start off with some examples of how other people had been able to resolve or mitigate risks?"

I hadn't, of course. He said it would have been a good way of getting everyone into a 'can-do' frame of mind.

"OK. But we really do need your help, Larry," I said. "We've got less than a week to sort all this lot out. It will probably take a couple of days to put the finishing touches to our proposal, and I need to allow some time for final checking before we print and bind the copies. And another thing – I've got Jean Cartwright on my back. Next Wednesday she wants to see all the facts and figures before they go to the chief exec. A thorough risk analysis, she says."

"I'm not surprised," Larry told me. "A business case ought to include a risk analysis. Personally, I'm not very keen on the complex kinds of plans that so often result from such a process. But I *am* keen on the process itself. It forces you to consider, right from the outset, the risks and the likely business implications of various options for managing them."

I could identify with Larry's philosophy. Rough-order-of-magnitude figures on an optimum approach would be better than a very detailed plan and an accurate estimate for doing the job inefficiently.

Rough-order-of-magnitude figures on an optimum approach are better than an accurate estimate for doing a job inefficiently

"Provided the right people are involved at the planning stage," Larry went on, "there is probably no better way of making sure that everyone has the same clear vision of what you are aiming to achieve. And that's a pretty solid foundation for building unity of purpose.

The clarity of vision and unity of purpose that come from the planning process are often worth more than the plans

"The danger is," Larry continued, "that the plan may become so detailed that only those involved in creating it stand any chance of understanding it. The plan can become an art form in its own right. Then you can get pitched battles between those who want to preserve the plan and those who want to get the job done."

"So what kind of plan do you suggest we include in our proposal to Bilstons?" I asked. "Should we let them see everything that we prepare for the chief exec?"

Larry told me that we should make a simple working plan that everyone in the team could understand and make use of. This would be very much along the lines of the plan to be included in the proposal to Bilstons, although in addition to the timescales we would also need cost targets in our working plan, of course. Then we should prepare whatever extra details the chief executive and the finance people would need before they could give us the go ahead.

"Bilstons will probably expect a monthly update," he suggested. "You won't be able to update your business case every month, but you will probably have to review it once a quarter, say."

"That doesn't sound too onerous. Is this how your division operates?"

Larry nodded. "I can let you see one of our risk- and opportunity-management plans, if you like. Use it as a template. It could save you a lot of time."

Then I told him about the real sticking point, the fact that our expected completion date was later than Bilstons were asking for.

After a few moments' thought, Larry told me that apart from bidding non-compliant we had three choices. We could cut the estimates, knowing that if we won the contract we were likely to let Bilstons down. I said that was the old way of working, and it had already cost us a great deal of credibility with customers. It wasn't an option, as far as I was concerned.

The second option was to start sooner. Bilstons would take at least two months to vet all the tenders and negotiate a contract, so if we started now we could be two months into the work by the time the order came in. There were two obstacles to that approach. We might not win, and then two months of work would be scrapped; and we were already strapped for cash. Without a down payment from Bilstons we couldn't fund the work.

"And what's the third option?" I asked.

"You make a better plan," he said. "So far you have only considered the risks. You also need to plan how you will manage the opportunities."

"You mean, something like that opportunity log you gave me to look at?" I asked.

He nodded.

"Well, I had a few difficulties with that. The risk register was full of things I could understand – things that could go wrong and would take time and cost money to put right. But . . ."

"The opportunity log was almost empty?" Larry interjected.

I nodded.

He said that you only need to develop your opportunity log to the point where you believe savings or additional benefits are achievable.

"Once you believe in the unicorn you can make it come true," he said. "Remember?"

I remembered, all right. But I explained that Jean wouldn't be happy unless I could provide her with facts and figures to back up my claims.

"Predicting the weather is very easy," he said. "Predicting big changes in the weather is the tricky bit."

I stared at him blankly.

"OK," he continued with a sigh. "Last year's performance levels aren't good enough to win you the Bilston contract. Right?" I nodded. "So Jean can't have provable facts and figures for everything. But don't worry, Jim. I think you will find her a lot more receptive as a result of last night's seminar. And before you ask – no. It wasn't anything I said. It was the old man. Gilbert Manning at full throttle is not something Jean Cartwright would want to stand in the way of."

"I wish I could have been there," I said.

"You'll get your chance," he replied. "Gilbert wants you to present the case study at our next session."

I felt the blood draining from my scalp. What if we lost the bid?

"Don't panic. It's not for three months. The contract will have been awarded by then and everyone will want to know how we won the order."

"I only hope you are right, Larry," I said. "But I wish we weren't going to be under the spotlight on such a high-risk bid."

"It is only by managing opportunity that you can expect to compensate for the inevitable setbacks in risky work," Larry said.

Only by managing opportunity can you compensate for the setbacks in risky work

"So you reckon we might still be able to meet the schedule target?"

"Oh yes, I would think so," he replied. "We'll have a clearer view once you have completed your risk-management plan. That will give us an idea of how much time-saving opportunity there is likely to be within the contract."

Larry showed me the cost plan his team had made for designing and setting up the new transport depot. The summary estimates were on spreadsheets, to which I had always cultivated a healthy aversion. (Often spreadsheets are nothing more than wild guesses dressed to appear as civilised facts.) This one looked simple enough, and as Larry talked me through the system it did make sense.

Milestone/Task/ Work Package	£k basic estimate	£k cost of unmitigated risk impact × Prob%	£k cost of counter- measures	£k cost of contingency plan Impact × Prob%	£k savings from risk-mg't plan
M1 – Design approved and accepted by client	37	12	4	5	3
M2 – Installation completed and approved	325	64	18	15	31
M3 – Warranty period completed	156	58	22	11	25
Totals:	518	134	44	31	59

For each of the key milestones, the spreadsheet listed the basic cost estimate excluding the effects of risk. Larry said that these milestones could correspond to the individual elements of a small assignment or the most significant steps to be achieved on a major project. Each milestone might involve several activities that contain risk, each of which would be recorded in the risk register. The risk register only listed the most significant risks, and most of these fell into the central region on the risk map.

I asked him how the list of risks was compiled. He said that at the initial risk-identification stage, as at subsequent reviews, it was crucial that the whole team should be involved in winkling out the threats to success; you rarely get a thorough assessment if it is left to just one person. (At least I had got that right: I had involved the whole team.)

The next column of figures also comes from the risk register and corresponds to the product of the additional cost expected if the risk materialises and the probability of its occurrence. The value of this product is your level of risk exposure. The way Larry explained it, if dozens of people were to carry out the same task taking no initiatives to counter the risks, then the unmitigated risk exposure is the mean value of the cost of sorting out the problems resulting from the risks (or, as can sometimes be the case, the loss suffered if no recovery action is feasible at that late stage). Put another way, the unmitigated risk exposure, added to the basic estimate, gives a realistic forecast of the cost and time to complete the job by crisis management.

The unmitigated risk exposure is the likely cost of dealing with risks by crisis management

"So broadly speaking the risk-exposure figure corresponds to the contingency budget in my own plan. Is that it?" I asked.

"In effect, yes," Larry agreed. "Not that I advocate crisis management as the preferred approach, you understand. But you do need a baseline against which to assess the value of proposed risk-mitigation counter-measures."

I nodded, and he continued: "On a big job you might have several pages of estimating and risk-assessment data. But that's no problem. The sub-totals just get carried forward to give a grand total for the particular milestone or phase of the work that you are planning."

I asked whether schedule risks are handled in the same way.

"Yes," he said. "But of course you are mainly concerned with any time extensions to tasks that fall on the critical path."

"You mean those parts of the work that follow one after the other and combine to determine the total duration of the job?" I queried.

"Yes, that's right," Larry agreed. "Any risks of schedule slip on the critical path need special attention because they can delay the whole job."

What we now had was a prediction of the outcome of tackling the work as if it contains no risks at all and then dealing reactively with anything that goes wrong. I felt very much at home with this kind of management: I had been practising it for years. But I also knew that there was a serious problem with this approach: you *never* have enough time, money and specialist resources in reserve to sort out the problems reactively, so you deliver late, infuriate your customer, overspend your budget and damage the business. Or you cut corners on quality and destroy your reputation altogether.

"So now let's look at the proactive part of the plan," Larry said.

There was that word again, proactive. I hoped this wasn't a prelude to another load of bureaucratic complexity.

Larry's telepathy receiver was tuned in. "Don't panic!" he told me. "It's not complicated."

As Larry explained it, you decide and record in the risk register how you intend reducing your risk exposure by taking counter-measures initiatives. You also estimate the cost of taking these initiatives. The idea is that you should save more time and money overall than you need to invest in the counter-measures – otherwise, crisis management or doing nothing at all would be better strategies. Schedule slip, loss of performance and erosion of market credibility can also be assessed in the same way.

As you are drawing up these plans, you will sometimes discover that what at first seemed to be an appropriate counter-measure isn't actually worth the time and money it costs. Or maybe it introduces new risks more serious than those you were trying to alleviate. So you use the risk register to record your final plan, but the process also helps you to decide between alternative ways of managing the most serious risks.

"And is that all there is to it?" I asked.

"For making the job more manageable by mitigating the major risks, yes," Larry said. "But I must stress that this is not a once-and-for-all task.

Risk assessment is not a once-and-for-all task, but an ongoing process

"As you learn more about the job and decide in detail how to do the work, you will probably avert or reduce some risks, come to realise that others are more serious than you first thought and need tackling in a different way from what you had planned, and maybe discover some new risks that require counter-measures, too. And often you find that some risks are purely imaginary and don't need the attention you at first thought they might. But as we will see shortly, you should also find or be able to create opportunities, and these can also cause you to change your management approach and your priorities.

"Having a proactive risk-management plan doesn't mean you have removed all risk," he continued. "You invariably find that some risk exposure remains even after planning your proactive counter-measures, and so you may need to work out your reactive risk-management approach. And this really *is* contingency planning. Do this initially in just enough detail to assign budgetary cost and time estimates. Then as the crunch point approaches refine your contingency plan – who is going to do what, when, where and how."

"Planning the panic before it happens!" I said cynically. "I would have thought there was quite enough detail in the plan already without another load of guesswork."

"Fair point," Larry conceded. "But let me ask *you* a question. How do *you* work out how much money and time to include in your budget for coping with crises?"

I had the answer to that one. "I've already told you. I try to build in 50 per cent for high-risk parts, 5 per cent for medium risks and 1 . . .

"All right," Larry interrupted, "but you also admitted that those figures always get cut back. Why do you think that happens?"

"Market forces, I suppose," I replied defensively.

"Market forces my foot!" he replied. "You get steam-rollered because you can't justify your figures."

He was right. Jean always asked the impossible: 'Prove it!' I could never get through to her that it was unreasonable to expect me to justify the figures when I've no idea what's going to go wrong and what we're going to have to do to put it right. But this argument cut no ice with Jean. I told Larry about it.

"Jean is probably right," he told me. "And that's what the reactive part of your risk-management plan is for. It's your way of justifying – to yourself as well as to senior management – the assumptions you make about the sorts of setbacks and crises that no amount of proactive management can reduce to zero."

"OK," I said. "Then perhaps you had better explain the reactive part of the plan. Let me guess – another great big spreadsheet? Jean would like that."

"You *could* keep it all on one huge spreadsheet if you wanted to. Personally, I prefer to have a window on just the data I need to concentrate on. So for planning purposes I continue to use the risk register and focus on specific risks. Then I include the totals – the management reserve – in the cost summary. It's up to you, Jim. But whichever way you choose, you need to assess and record the residual risk exposure after allowing for your proactive counter-measures. Mostly, the nature of the risk will be unchanged with only its impact or its probability being altered. But you might occasionally introduce new risks associated with your proactive counter-measures."

"For example?" I prompted.

Larry thought for a moment. "Remember the paratrooper?" he asked. "Fitting a second parachute brings in the new risk that the two 'chutes might become entangled such that both fail to open."

"So, let's see if I've got this right," I said. "The proactive counter-measures are a means of reducing the initial risk exposure. But they must be worthwhile after taking into account any new risks they might introduce. Overall, this means the savings in terms of reduced risk exposure have to be greater than the cost of the counter-measures. Is that the idea?"

"That's right," Larry confirmed. "So now you are ready to make a reactive plan – your contingency plan, if you like – for those risks that remain even after your proactive counter-measures."

He explained that the reactive plan is a summary, in the risk register, of how each residual risk will be dealt with if it materialises. This reactive work has to be assessed both in terms of its cost and its duration, and as before you have to make a judgement as to the likelihood of the residual risk occurring – 50, 5 or 1 per cent, for instance, unless you can get a more precise figure from your historical records.

"Oh yes," I interjected. "Now I see. By multiplying the probability of a crisis reaction being necessary with the estimated cost of the extra work, you get the final cost risk exposure." Larry nodded, and I continued: "And then, if the risk is on the critical path, you get the final schedule risk exposure by multiplying the probability by the schedule delay that would be caused by the crisis. That's pretty straightforward."

Larry agreed. He said that the management reserve was an estimate of the money and time that would be needed over and above the 'if-all-goes-to-plan' figures in the baseline estimate. These costs and time extensions are not allocated to milestones, individual tasks or work packages; they are a central reserve to be used as and when risks materialise and extra resources and time are needed to resolve them.

I could certainly see the sense in retaining centrally a reactive risk-management reserve. If there was a 10 per cent chance of needing an extra month on a task, allocating three days to deal with the crisis would be no use at all. You would either need nothing at all or a full month.

The whole process seemed painfully bureaucratic, but there was nothing in the maths that frightened me. My people would be able to cope with it (although I could expect moans and groans from Pete) and I was sure we *could* do it this way. But would it actually *help*?

"It certainly will help. Believe me," Larry said earnestly. "But only if you put real thought into the risk-management plan. It's crucially important to work out the best ways of reducing your exposure to risk without overburdening the estimate with unnecessary costs and delays. Keep the plan simple so that *you* can concentrate on the difficult bit – keeping on target by managing the risks rather than slavishly following a very detailed plan."

Keep the plan simple so that you can concentrate on the difficult bit – keeping on target

"Fair enough," I said. "I can see that you might reduce your risk exposure by proactive initiatives. And I accept that you'll never remove all the risk, so some sort of contingency fund will be needed. But how can you be so sure that you have found the best way of going about reducing the level of risk in a job?"

"I'm not saying you can," he replied. "But at least with this approach you can compare options and see what payoff you are likely to get from your investment in proactive counter-measures. When you compare the estimates for the wait-and-see, crisis-management option with the totals predicted from your risk-management plan, you can see how much time and money you are likely to save."

Larry paused to see that I was getting the drift. I nodded, and he continued: "One other point before we leave the reactive part of the plan. You probably won't be able to find counter-measures for every major risk. You may find that some of them have to be managed entirely reactively or, in the worst case, that there is absolutely nothing at all you can do and you just have to accept the consequences. Only if you have no option would you take an approach to a job that leaves you as exposed as this."

"Is that the only time you would recommend reactive risk management as a first-line response?" I asked.

"I'm afraid not," he said. "Remember the risk map? You will be relying on your contingency plans for all risks that fall below the diagonal line. Where you draw that line is largely determined by the resources you have available. For obvious reasons, you would start with the most serious risks and go down the list until you have dealt with them all – or, in practice, until you have no more resources available to deploy in risk mitigation. You will have to manage some of the lower exposure risks reactively. The reactive part of your risk-management summary helps the organisation to budget for the extra resources you will need to deal with problems as they arise."

"Hang on, Larry!" I said. "Did I hear that right? Budget for *yet more* resources to carry out the reactive risk-management plan? But that will put up my baseline estimate even further."

"No. You need to plan for the extra resources, time and money, but they don't go into the baseline estimate. They go into the management reserve. They are notional allowances for reactive risk management – a bit like your contingencies but, if you don't mind me saying so, with logic behind the figures."

I couldn't argue with any of that, but I was becoming more uneasy by the minute: to increase our chances of winning the contract we ought to be *reducing* our estimate. And we definitely had to cut back on the schedule; we were still a long way off what Bilstons expected. But I had no better ideas of my own.

Larry said that you have to be particularly careful with schedule risks. If things go badly wrong on what should have been a non-critical part of the job, the critical path can alter. If you want to investigate these sorts of possibilities you need to do a 'what if' analysis. On big jobs with lots of risks, you might need to use a computer for this analysis.

Ours wasn't such a big job, so I wasn't going to get drawn down that particular avenue. But I was interested in what happens to the management reserve and who actually has it. Larry said that the reserve might not even exist. Its main purpose is to highlight the level of risk inherent in the job. If you bid a very low price to win an order from an external customer, the management reserve might even exceed the profit margin. But at least you have given your organisation fair warning of the costs likely to be incurred on top of the 'if-all-goes-to-plan' estimate.

Next I asked what you can do if the forecast duration is unacceptably long or the cost estimates including risk allowance come out way above what would be a winning price. He explained that although the proactive counter-measures foreseen at the initial planning stage should yield *some* forecast savings in cost and overall duration, this only helps set the baseline estimate and is *not* the target figure. Targets for opportunity management are also necessary, and they are the means of bridging the gap between the estimates and the required budget.

Opportunity management is the means of bridging the gap between the estimates and the required budget

"Well, I'll have to take your word for that, Larry," I said. "But at least I now understand the basics of risk management. Let me check one thing, though. You say I should include the cost of the proactive risk-management activities – the counter-measures – in the baseline estimate. Is that normal?"

"It's *essential*," Larry said. "These are things you definitely intend doing so that the job becomes more manageable. You will need both the time and the resources to carry out your proactive plan – otherwise, you might as well not bother to make a plan."

The cost of risk-management counter-measures is part of the baseline estimate

"Right, I can see the logic of that. One thing still bothers me, though. So far, everything you have told me to do is going to put *up* the estimate for the job. As I told you earlier, we desperately need to get our costs *down*, not up."

Larry said that, whatever the cost, it would almost certainly be higher if we went ahead without a proactive plan for managing risk. And he said that in the planning process it is important to assess the cost of each action against the benefits it provides in terms of reduced exposure to risks, and particularly the risks of schedule and cost overrun.

The cost is almost always higher if you go ahead without a proactive plan for managing risk

"Don't begrudge the time and effort spent on this," he urged. "It can save you a lot more time and money later. But remember, you do need to consider alternative ways of managing a risk – this is the most valuable step in the whole process."

Considering alternative ways of managing a risk is a crucial step in the process

"Good managers don't simply plump for the first solution they come across," he emphasised.

Myth
Faced with a problem, a manager's job is to find a solution

"Your job is to select the best solution from a wide range of options," Larry continued, "especially when you are planning how to manage the most serious risks."

Good problem solving means choosing the best from a range of solutions – including the 'do nothing' option

"OK," I said. "But I really must bring you back to the issue I raised a few minutes ago. Everything that you've suggested is going to push up our cost estimates. I still need to cut costs and get the job done more quickly."

"Risks always push up costs. So, naturally, a risk assessment is likely to push up the baseline estimate, not to mention highlighting the need for a risk-management reserve. But if you need to make savings, it's the basic estimate that you should be looking to improve on."

"Ah! Then I've been doing it right after all," I told him. "I've already had to slash the estimates on the Bilston bid. The trouble is, if we produce a proper risk-management plan I can see the totals shooting back up to where they were, if not higher."

"Perhaps you're right. Perhaps whoever wins the Bilston order is going to make a crashing loss on the deal. If you're not clear about the budget, maybe you shouldn't bid for it."

"I didn't say that, Larry. I'm pretty sure that our assessment of the customer's budget isn't so far out. Unfortunately I'm not at all sure we can do the job within the budget."

"So, what *is* included in your cost target?" he asked.

"The cost of doing the work, of course," I answered.

"What work?"

I was getting a bit tired of this continual barrage of questions. "Do you really want me to go through all the details right now?" I asked.

"No. What I was trying to establish is what sorts of things are included in and what are excluded from your target. Would it help if I showed you how we work out our own cost targets?"

I had a feeling it would help a lot. I nodded. "Over a coffee?"

Larry redrew the sketch he had shown me when we first began discussing risk and opportunity – the one showing the components of an estimate. He added more detail to the block allocated to 'Fund for dealing with risks'. This time he broke it into its two components, one for proactive risk management and the other for reactive risk management.

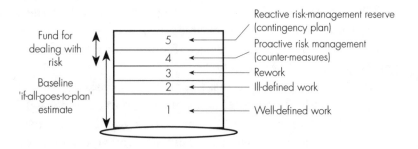

Larry reminded me what each of the blocks represented. "You'll remember that the first chunk of your estimate is for the

well-defined things you know for sure will have to be done.
Then there are other things that will have to be done but are ill-
defined because you don't have a perfect vision of the future.
Block three is an allowance for work that has to be done again
because of mistakes. Blocks four and five are for risk management. There are the proactive risk-management activities, or
counter-measures initiatives – things you intend doing over and
above the basic minimum so that risks are less likely to
materialise or, if they do, they will have less impact and be more
manageable. And then – "

"And then there is a reactive risk-management reserve," I
interjected. "I know all about that, and I now understand *why*
you keep it separate from the baseline estimate. You don't
distribute it across the milestones, work packages or tasks
because you cannot be sure exactly where it will be needed. But
it is the final element of the estimate as far as the business is
concerned."

"Final on *that side* of the equation, yes," Larry said, leaning
back in his chair. He moved his elbow, and I saw that he had
placed all these components of the estimate on one side of a
weighing scales. On the other side there was another set of
components.

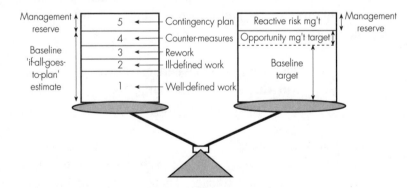

"Where did you get *this* lot from?" I demanded.

Larry read the confusion on my face. "Don't panic. There's
nothing to worry about," he reassured me. "The only difference

here is that the new baseline cost target is the basic estimate *minus* the opportunity-management target."

"Excuse me," I said. "Opportunity-management target? Where did you magic that from? I can see that if you subtract from the basic estimate a thumping great amount called the opportunity-management target you will get a reduced estimate. The difficulty I'm having, Larry, is that there hasn't been so much as a mention of opportunity-management targets until now, and suddenly you throw in this bombshell. Come to think of it, I'm more convinced than ever that I've been doing the right thing all along, albeit maybe for the wrong reasons. I *have been* subtracting a great chunk of cost from the estimates in order to get to a competitive figure. What's the difference?"

"The difference – and it is a very important difference – is that your slashing of the estimates is arbitrary while mine is based on an opportunity-management plan. Arbitrary pruning of their estimates is guaranteed to demotivate your team and nip creativity in the bud.

Arbitrary pruning of estimates can nip creativity in the bud

"On the other hand, a realistic gap between estimate and target is a challenge to the creative thinking of the team who will be doing the work."

A realistic gap between estimate and target is a challenge to creative thinking

I had no answer to that.

"Don't sulk," Larry said. "You are probably doing the right thing in cutting back your estimates. There can be sound reasons for doing so."

"Really?"

"Sure! You need to reduce the amount of rework – a euphemism for waste and inefficiency. And you also need to increase the effectiveness of your business. Cutting estimates for future work is your commitment to achieving these goals."

Opportunity-management targets are a commitment to improving efficiency and effectiveness

"I see," I said, and then: "No – I really don't see."

Reducing the level of scrap and rework I could understand. We had been trying to do this for years. At first the savings had been impressive, but latterly there didn't seem to be much mileage in the process of continuous improvement based on efficiency savings. In our business it had come down to laying off people every year and sharing their work across the overloaded few who were left. If anything, it was leading to *more* mistakes, *more* scrapped materials and *more* rework. Improving effectiveness sounded much more interesting, and I asked Larry to tell me more about it.

"It means a better deal for your staff, for the owners of the business, for key suppliers, for all of your stakeholders," he said. "You do this by giving your customers higher quality and better value for money every year. You should know all about that, Jim. You work in the electronics sector, which is way ahead of the rest of industry in this respect."

I said I couldn't see that we deserved any bouquets.

Larry told me about his meeting with the woman whose job it was to buy personal computers for the company. She had said that value for money was increasing at a rate of around 5 per cent per month, and you don't make those kinds of savings by getting everyone to reuse paper clips. Such improvements can only come from continual innovation – real opportunity management.

You are unlikely to achieve great leaps in productivity by getting everyone to reuse paper clips

"Take any other example you like," Larry said. "A television set, for argument's sake. Over the past thirty years the price of a TV has more than halved, and in real terms today's price is a mere fraction of what you would have paid three decades ago. But at the same time, what you get in terms of features, performance and reliability has increased beyond recognition. Continuous improvement is an inescapable requirement in most jobs nowadays, including ours. We have to look for opportunities to become more effective."

Opportunity management is the cornerstone of a strategy for continuous improvement

"Right," I said. "So you're saying that if we are to work within tighter budgets and shorter time schedules every year then we have to improve efficiency *and* effectiveness, and this means reducing rework – getting more of the work right first time – and managing opportunity. Reducing rework I can understand, but what does opportunity management really mean in practice?"

"It can mean any number of things. For example, finding improved ways of doing things. Better, faster, cheaper. There's no simple formula for opportunity management. It requires imagination and initiative. But it *is* something you can plan."

There's no simple formula for opportunity management, but it is something you can plan

I was keen to do all that, but I wasn't at all sure how to go about it.

"I still need your help, Larry. Will you show us how we can make an opportunity-management plan for the Bilston job?"

"Tell you what," he said. "Let's get the team together and draw up a risk-management plan to convince Jean and the chief exec that you know what you're doing. Then by all means we can meet again – a quite separate session, mind you – and I'll try to help you make an opportunity-management plan."

"Thanks, Larry. That's great," I told him with a wry smile. "*You* might as well finish what *we've* not even been able to start."

"OK," he replied. "But the plan is not the *finish* of anything – it's only the start. It's important to have a good plan when you set the targets for a job. The right sort of plan can be very useful when you come to do the work. It can help you make good management decisions. In practice, however, very few plans *are* good. And even fewer actually get used."

One of the biggest risks with any plan is the risk that no one will use it

"That's one thing we *are* good at," I said. "Our basic plan is pretty sound. And so it ought to be. It took ages to prepare."

For some reason this didn't seem to convince Larry. "I think it might be a good idea if you and I got together before the team meeting," he said. "I need to understand how you intend tackling this job. Bring the plan with you and talk me through it. Half an hour should be plenty of time. Tomorrow morning, when we're both fresh?" I nodded. "And set the team session for eleven, so we can run through until lunch if necessary."

For the first time in weeks I felt reasonably satisfied with the way things were going, and so it was with a feeling of optimism that I sat down that evening to update my notebook. I had picked up a lot of useful ideas about planning to manage risk and opportunity.

Subject: Making a risk-management plan

- The first step towards innovation is imitation.
- The clarity of vision and unity of purpose that come from the planning process are often more valuable than the plan itself.
- By managing opportunity you can often compensate for the inevitable setbacks in risky work.
- Risk assessment is not a once-and-for-all task, but an ongoing process.
- Opportunity management is the means of bridging the gap between the estimates and the required budget.
- The cost is almost always higher if you go ahead without a proactive plan for managing risk.
- Good problem solving means choosing the best from a range of solutions – including the 'do nothing' option.
- Arbitrary pruning of estimates can nip creativity in the bud.
- A realistic gap between estimate and target is a challenge to creative thinking.
- Opportunity-management targets are a commitment to improving efficiency and effectiveness.
- Proactive risk management usually costs money and may take time, but it reduces the risk of incurring far greater costs and delays later.
- You are unlikely to achieve great leaps in productivity by getting everyone to reuse paper clips.
- There is no simple formula for opportunity management, but it is something you can plan.
- One of the biggest risks with any plan is the risk that no one will use it.

Action: Now that I understand what a good plan should be, I must make one and use it to help make good decisions.

Chapter 7

Harnessing the unicorn:
turning risk into opportunity

First thing on Friday morning I was in Larry's office, and I was feeling anxious. Larry had been silent for too long. He was no longer looking at the plan but staring at the wall above my head.

"This is just the overview plan," I reminded him. "The key milestones and the major tasks throughout the programme. There are lots more details if you would like to see them. In fact it's probably the most thorough plan we've ever made. We know exactly how we are going to do every part of the job, right through the whole programme of work."

"You don't *mean* that, do you?" Larry asked. He looked worried.

"Absolutely!" I told him. "It's a massive chart covering almost a complete wall of my office. Come and see it if you don't believe me. Jean thinks it's great. Everything is planned and scheduled right down to the smallest detail. It took us ages, but at least everyone knows exactly what they're supposed to do and how they're supposed to do it."

Larry frowned and stared hard at something obnoxious in the basement three floors below us. "No, no. I believe you, Jim. It's just that your plan can only show how you *would have* done the job in the past," he told me. "It may be a reasonable basis for estimating how long it *would have* taken you and how much money you *would have* spent.

Activity plans merely show how you *would have* done the work in the past

"But if you use this as a means of deciding in detail on your activities too far into the future, its simply a recipe for losing any competitive edge you might once have had."

"But we've got no choice," I insisted. "All jobs have got to have a cost and implementation plan. You know that. We have to look forward."

Larry frowned again. "That's true. But you do understand the difference between an estimate and a target, don't you?" He stared at me hard.

"Well . . ." I said and then stopped. I could have added more words but no more meaning.

"Estimates are based on experience," he said. "Which means hindsight. Target setting is for the future, and it requires foresight."

Estimating is based on hindsight; target setting requires foresight

"Listen," I said. "How can I say whether a target is realistic if I don't have an estimate of what the work is going to cost?" Larry was shaking his head. "Oh, all right," I conceded. "If you want to be pedantic, an estimate of what it *would have* cost if we had already done it."

"You're missing the point, Jim," Larry said. "Estimates invariably presume we will carry on doing things the way we have in the past. Targets involve an intention to become more efficient and more effective – to become better at some of the things we do and to find better ways of doing other things."

Estimates presume we will perform as in the past; targets imply an intention to improve

"Good point," I said weakly. "But so what?"

Larry explained that the plan ought to start with a summary of what you aim to achieve. From this you work out the key achievement steps along the way – the milestones. These aren't the activities or the tasks you intend doing. They're not even the completion of major tasks. They should be what you intend achieving: a state reached by whatever turns out to be the most effective means. You decide the ways and means – such as what exactly to do, who will do it, and how – progressively. At the outset, a good plan has all its key milestones defined (as we had tried to do) but only the first few weeks of work are usually mapped out in full detail. You roll this planning process forward progressively so that, as you approach new milestones and begin working on new tasks, the resources and methods of working are agreed and prepared. Prescribing too much detail too far in advance simply precludes innovation. It acts as an obstacle to opportunity management.

Prescribing too much detail too far in advance is an obstacle to opportunity management and innovation

We agreed that our risk-assessment workshop should concentrate on the overall objective, the key milestones and the major tasks we would have to carry out in the early weeks of the contract. And at this point we broke off our discussions, organised coffee and called in the rest of the team.

I had expected to be getting down to the risk-assessment work right away, but Larry said that we should start by tackling a warm-up exercise to get used to the process. The scenario was this: we had to imagine we needed to get all five team members from one side of an estuary to the other at a point where the river was about forty yards wide and up to six feet deep. Our supplies consisted of empty sixty-gallon barrels, rope, planks, hammers, nails and the like. Every item carried a cost. Larry was all for making the crossing for real, later, to see just how good our risk-management plan really was. Pete was keen; everyone else wanted to keep the exercise theoretical.

First we had to produce a basic estimate, and that led to an argument about the design of our raft: two barrels or four? Larry let us battle it out for a while and then asked why we were using multiples of two. Always the one for compromise, Nadia suggested three barrels, three planks and lots of rope to lash it all together. We worked out our costs and agreed they seemed reasonable.

"And the timescale?" Larry asked.

"Twenty minutes to build it and ten minutes to cross the river," Pete proposed. None of us had ever built a raft before, and Pete sounded confident so we went along with his figures.

"Excellent progress," Larry said. "You made short work of that. Now then. How risky is it?"

"Very!" Jill said emphatically. "Unless we have at least one barrel per person I'm not going on it."

"Nobody's going on it!" Pete retorted. "I was outvoted, so it's only a theoretical exercise. Remember? If money's no object, we could have dozens of barrels. But I thought we were supposed to be trying to do the job at minimum cost."

"Are we?" Larry asked.

"Well, *you* made up the exercise," I said. "Why don't *you* tell *us*!"

"OK," Larry said, with a hint of sarcasm. "By all means let's agree the goal – now that you've decided on your plan."

A chill silence fell on the room. We had made the most basic of planning errors: choosing our solution before considering the criteria for success.

Larry broke the silence. "Suppose lowest cost consistent with a safe crossing is your goal. What then?"

"Well," Jill said. "I suppose we should go for the minimum

number of barrels we can make a raft from. They're by far the most expensive items. Perhaps two would be enough."

We each sketched our own designs and then together we assessed the options. There wasn't a lot of variety in concept. The main differences were in the positioning of the planks and how the thing was to be held together. We quickly agreed on a hybrid version.

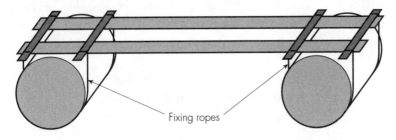

Fixing ropes

Larry watched, waited and scribbled on his notepad. I sensed that he was finding it hard to resist the temptation to interject his own ideas.

When we had finished he said: "OK, stay with that design, but I think you might have considered more alternatives. How about a one-barrel raft?" And he showed us the sketch he had been making.

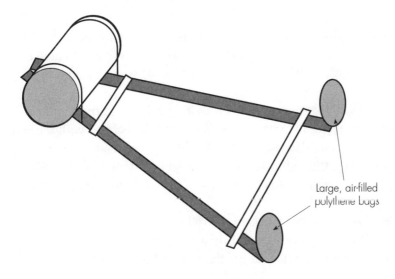

Large, air-filled polythene bags

"Surely that wouldn't take five people," Jill said.

"No, probably not," Larry replied. "But it would be able to take one person at a time. You're not after the fastest crossing, but you do need the lowest possible cost. That is your goal, remember."

Pete glanced around the group and said: "Oh well, we all assumed the raft had to take five people, didn't we?"

"Don't let assumptions relating to what you *might* do cloud your vision of what you need to achieve," Larry said. "Otherwise you will surely miss some important opportunities."

Don't let assumptions relating to what you *might* do cloud your vision of what you *must* achieve

"Now, let's get on with the risk assessment," Larry said. "What are the risks?"

"The raft," Pete suggested.

"Yes. And the river, of course," Jill added.

"They are *sources* of risk, I agree," Larry said. "But what *are* the risks? What could go wrong?"

After some discussion we came up with three significant risks:

- The raft might sink if it has insufficient buoyancy.
- The raft might fall apart if our knots aren't good enough.
- The raft might capsize if its centre of gravity is too high.

Larry said that we ought to consider the dynamic risks – those to do with using the raft – as well as those associated with the raft construction. He said we should try to picture ourselves struggling through estuary mud to launch the raft and paddle it across the river. That helped us to indentify four more risks:

- We might get stuck in the mud.
- We might run aground on a sand bank.
- Someone might fall off the raft and get swept out to sea.

- The raft itself might get swept out to sea if the current is too strong.

Next we each took one of the risks, filled out a risk register page, and presented our ideas to the rest of the team.

Pete worked out the buoyancy of two barrels and said that they would be quite capable of taking all five of us if necessary. Nadia checked the sums and agreed. Then Larry produced a couple of 35 mm film canisters and said we could build a scale model in a matter of minutes if any of us still had doubts. This, he said, was an example of a proactive counter-measure that would cost almost nothing but might help us save a great deal of time and trouble later.

Ten minutes later we had prototyped three different designs and tested them in a bowl of water, loading them with Plasticine people. Larry's single-barrel raft was considerably more stable than our two-barrel design, which kept toppling over until we fitted outriggers at yet more expense.

When we were all happy that the risk of capsizing had been reduced to negligible, we turned our attention to some of the dynamic risks, beginning with the prospect of getting stuck in the mud.

"As I see it, we have a choice," Pete said. "We can either buy plenty of spare rope so that we can throw it to whoever gets stuck and the rest of us can haul them free. Or – and bearing in mind that cost is the key target this would be my preference – we can go and buy some rope if, and only if, the need arises."

Jill glowered at him. "Typical crisis management!" she said.

"Stick-in-the-mud," he retorted, and even Jill couldn't suppress a grin. It was, after all, only a theoretical exercise.

"OK, so what about the risk of being swept out to sea?" I asked. "Any ideas, Nadia?"

"We could attach a long rope, so if the raft began drifting out to sea someone on the bank could pull it back," she suggested. "We would need at least fifty metres of rope – how much would that cost?"

"Wait a minute," Dave said. "Why not wait until slack water around high or low tide? Then we wouldn't have a problem with the current."

"Good idea," Jill said. "High tide, for preference. That way we wouldn't have to wade through the mud to get to the water's edge. And we would also avoid the risk of getting stuck on a sand bank."

"That's it," Nadia said. "We need tide tables. You know, sailors and fishermen use them. They tell you when it is high tide at different places along the coast. Then we wouldn't have to hang around waiting for slack water."

"Excellent!" Larry said. "Your proactive counter-measures will reduce the risk exposure enormously. And I'm sure you could work out how to deal with the other risks, too. The ideas are more important than the estimates at this stage. The more options you can generate the better. We won't bother to do the sums; I'm sure you could all work out the costings and time estimates."

"Actually, I wouldn't mind completing this," Pete said. "I'm quite enjoying it."

"Me too," Jill agreed. "With a plan like this I *might* even be willing to join you on the expedition."

Larry said that constructing a really good risk-management plan, one that everyone contributes to and understands, is an invaluable step towards securing team commitment to any risky venture.

A good risk-management plan that everyone contributes to is an invaluable step towards securing team commitment

Then it was time to turn our attention to the Bilston contract. We listed the risk areas within each of the major milestones and the key tasks that we thought they might entail. As in the case of the raft, where capsizing wasn't an issue with the single-barrel solution but was a serious concern with our two-barrel design, the level (and sometimes the very nature) of the risk depended on what we decided to do to meet the objectives and how we intended going about it.

It took us two hours to complete our first draft of the risk register. We incorporated proactive counter-measures for most of the major risks, and agreed contingency plans where necessary. One particular risk that gave us a bit of bother at first was to do with the new antenna mast. We had estimated that installing the base, a steel-reinforced concrete and brickwork building, would cost £55 000 and take sixteen weeks if all went well. There was a risk that the foundations would need piling – there had been a land slip some eighty years earlier, thought to be due to cavitation caused by an underground stream. (There was nothing on any maps to help us, but we were aware that a small stream emerged in a rocky gully half a mile to the north.) Subsidence during construction we could deal with; subsidence afterwards would affect antenna alignment, and if that happened we thought it could take five weeks to sort out the problem at an additional cost of around £25 000. Our best guess (based on our rather limited experience of this kind of work) was that there was a 20 per cent chance of subsidence occurring. The unmitigated risk exposure was therefore:

$$0.2 \times £25000 = £5000$$

Added to the 'if-all-goes-well' estimate, this gave an expected completion cost of £60 000.

By starting the foundation work early enough we could avoid any schedule impact, and so cost was the critical factor in this part of the job. Any counter-measures and contingency actions would have to cost less than £5000 in order to be preferable to 'wait-and-see' crisis management.

We came up with two proactive measures to reduce the risk exposure. The first suggestion was to survey the site and choose a safe location for the antenna base. The survey would cost us about £1000. Of course, no survey is perfect and there would still be a small chance of subsidence. We assessed this residual risk as having a 5 per cent chance of occurring, leaving us with 5 per cent of £25 000 = £1250 as our residual risk exposure.

The expected cost of doing this element of the work using option one was therefore:

Basic 'if-all-goes-well' estimate	£55000	
Proactive counter-measures costs	£1000	
Baseline estimate		£56000
Reactive risk-management reserve		£1250
Expected total cost		£57250

This approach offered an expected saving of £60 000 − £57 250 = £2750 compared with 'wait-and-see' management.

The alternative solution meant rather more work. It would involve installing automatic servos to stabilise the platform against subsidence; these would cost some £4500 but provided two major advantages. The first was that the extra work could be done in parallel with other activities and so would not delay completion of the job; and second, it enabled us to relax the specification for the foundations, giving a cost saving of £3500. The net cost of the servos was therefore only £1000. The residual risk of antenna misalignment was negligible and so we felt no need for any contingency plan or reactive management reserve.

The expected cost of doing this element of the work using option two was therefore:

Basic 'if-all-goes-well' estimate	£55000	
Proactive counter-measures costs (net)	£1000	
Baseline estimate		£56000
Reactive risk-management reserve		£0
Expected total cost		£56000

This was the approach we chose.

We went through the top ten risks in this way. Overall we planned to spend an extra £14 300 and to extend the programme by two weeks in order to carry out our proactive counter-measures to mitigate risk. The benefit from all this was a forecast reduction in reactive risk-management costs of £38 500 – an overall forecast saving of £24 200 compared with 'wait-and-see' crisis management.

Even so, I was concerned that we were increasing our baseline estimate to cover the cost of the counter-measures, but Larry reminded me that whatever we would have spent working to our original plan the new approach was likely to cost us some £24 000 less. We also made a forecast schedule saving of five weeks, although that still left us somewhat adrift of where we needed to be.

Next, we plotted the positions on the risk chart of the top ten cost risks before and after proactive mitigation; most had been reduced significantly in impact, in probability or in both.

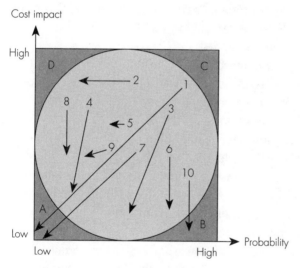

We all agreed that the new plan was a good one. Larry said that once we got the contract (he didn't say 'if', and this encouraged the team) we would need to look ahead continually for improved ways of countering the risks. As our view of later milestones and tasks became clearer, we would need to review the risk register. This, he stressed, was a major source of opportunity.

**As your view of the objectives
becomes clearer, improving
your risk counter-measures is a
major source of opportunity**

With no risk allowance, the basic if-all-goes-well estimate for
the Bilston contract was a seventy-nine-week programme of
work. The proactive mitigation measures had extended it by two
weeks, and our best estimate of the residual schedule risk
exposure was a further four weeks. That gave us an eighty-five-
week forecast time to completion – nearly two months longer
than Bilstons were asking for, but at least it was a programme I
could justify.

After lunch I typed up the results and by mid-afternoon I was
able to take them along to show Jean. After a perfunctory glance
at our figures she said: "Seems reasonable. Does it fit in with the
schedule Bilstons are asking for?"

"Not quite," I replied.

"Then it's *un*reasonable," she retorted irritably.

(Where was the changed attitude that Larry thought he had
brought about overnight?)

"We're still working on the details," I told her. "We're doing
an opportunity-management plan on Monday. With a bit of luck
it should be OK when we've finished."

"Listen Jim. I'm not prepared to pin my future on luck. It's
got to fit. For certain. When it does I'll approve it, but not until
I've seen all the figures. I need to know what risk we are going
to be taking," she said.

"What? You mean you want *even more* details?"

"You bet! How can I make a decision without all the facts and
figures?"

"But you don't understand," I blurted. "Look! These *are* the
risks, all listed neatly. And here – these are the risk-management
actions we intend to take. These *are* the facts. What *more* do you
want?"

"Facts *and figures*, Jim. On all the risks. These are just the top
ten. There must be more. Something like this might be OK for

including in the proposal. All Bilstons need to know is that we have considered the major risks and we know how we're going to manage them. But I need to be sure you're not going to cripple the business by making a crashing loss on this contract. I need to see all the facts *and* figures."

"We've allowed for all the risks and we've worked out how we want to manage the major ones. If this isn't good enough, what *do* you want?" I pressed, beginning to feel like a student who had blundered into the wrong examination room. "You tell me what you want, Jean, then I'll tell you whether I can do it by Wednesday."

"Well, for a start, about these risks – I really ought to check that you have got them all in the right categories," Jean said.

"Larry's done all that," I said irritably. "Surely you don't need to buy a dog and then bark yourself!"

"All right," she conceded. "If Larry's checked the figures that's fine by me. But you don't seriously expect me to believe that these are the *only* risks, do you? There must be others. How serious are they? What exactly do you propose to do about them? And what will *that* do to the overall cost and timescale? Even if you don't intend showing Bilstons that much detail, *I* need to see it."

"OK. But we've done all that. And we've got a risk map to prove it, and part of the baseline estimate is earmarked for dealing reactively with the minor risks and ill-defined work. We've got a lot more information than is shown in the plan. If you want a more detailed plan than this one, that's fine. But can't we finish it after the bid has gone off to Bilstons? I don't think the team will be amused if I ask them to work *another* Saturday. It's over a month since any of them had a full weekend off."

Jean sighed and sat back in her chair. "Listen, Jim," she said, in the sort of voice I imagined she reserved for telling her children why they could not have junkburgers for dinner every day. "Just be clear on one thing. When you come to me with a plan that falls patently short of our customer's expectations, and you tell me I don't need to look at the fine details, you are effectively asking me to abdicate my duty, and . . ."

"I'm not," I interrupted.

"You *are*! And I'm not going to."

I felt a sullen scowl take control of my face muscles.

"You really must understand," she went on, "you and your team who value your precious weekends so highly. If we lose the Bilston bid it's a fair bet that by next spring some of us won't see any difference between weekdays and weekends. And include you and me in the list. I'm not trying to pressure anyone unduly, but we've got to win this order. And to do that we've first got to convince the chief that we can deliver on time and at a profit. If he decides not to bid – and he could still do that, you know . . ."

"OK," I said. I had got the message. "But I've already told you we'll be working with Larry on Monday morning to see if we can find opportunities to trim the costs and the schedule. Meanwhile, as far as the proposal is concerned, it would help me to know that you are happy with the way we are approaching it."

"Good," Jean said. "You've shown me. So now I know. But don't expect me to say I'm happy when I'm not. I'm not ungrateful. I do appreciate what you and your people are doing. But I won't be happy until you can show me that the work fits into the schedule Bilstons are asking for."

That was typical of Jean. She wasn't interested in *us*. All that mattered to her was *what we were doing*. It never dawned on her that people might need to feel that *they* were appreciated, too. If only she could have spared a few minutes to see the team – to thank them personally. They would have appreciated that.

"Well *I* think the team have done a *great* job," I said emphatically, defying her to claim otherwise. "It's not going to be a pushover, but if all goes well I think we can still make it," I added lamely.

"When did *you* last have a job go well?" she retorted.

She had a point. Our improved plan only made it clearer that if we won the contract we would probably be two months late in completing the work.

"Plan with pessimism; manage with optimism," I said. "We have got a proper plan for dealing with the risks. That's something we've never had before."

"All right, if you're so sure none of our competitors will be able to offer the completion date Bilstons are asking for, we've nothing to worry about. Is that what you're saying? We bid non-compliant on completion date and you put your job on the line if we lose the order? You must be supremely confident in the gospel according to Saint Larry. That's all I can say."

It was a trap. Jean knew as well as I did that we had no chance of winning the contract unless we could offer completion by the date Bilstons were asking for. But equally, I had no intention of simply reducing the schedule estimates and imposing impossible targets on the team.

"There's nothing wrong with the thinking behind these figures, Jean," I told her. "That's not to say someone else couldn't come up with a tighter schedule. Someone with more support from their senior management, perhaps."

"And what's *that* supposed to mean?" Jean demanded. She was getting rattled. I had touched a raw spot. Good!

"Simply this," I said. "We all realise that to no-bid this job isn't an option. Not if we want to stay in business. That's why the whole team are putting in the hours right now. But what are *you* contributing? You never offer to contribute to our planning sessions. You even seem to resent the fact that we're getting help from Larry Farlow. Surely you don't see him as a threat to your position."

Jean glowered but said nothing, and I continued, "Believe me, without Larry's help we probably *would* have produced a schedule that matched the Bilston delivery requirements . . ." A puzzled expression flickered across Jean's face, and she turned away from her computer to face me. I pressed on regardless: "And we would have had absolutely no chance of keeping our promises. Instead of which I come to you with a genuine problem where we've done absolutely everything we can think of, and what help do you offer? Nothing. Just criticism. We don't need it, Jean. Why can't you give us some real support when we need it?"

Jean's face changed from pink, to red, to blue. I thought she was going to burst her boiler.

"To take your questions in turn, Jim," she said in quiet, hissing monotone. "First, I'm not an expert in the sort of work Bilstons want. You are. Or at least you're supposed to be. That's why we employ you. Second, you asked me to let you arrange for some of Larry Farlow's time. I agreed. It was I who got Gilbert Manning to have a word with Larry's boss and make sure there wasn't going to be a problem there. Now you're saying that the idea hasn't been a success . . ."

"I'm *not* saying that," I interrupted. "All I'm saying is . . ."

"Do you want me to answer your questions or not?" she snapped. I said nothing, and she went on: "As for assessing whether the schedule you have produced is acceptable or not, that *is* part of my job. Do you seriously expect me to sign it off without looking at the figures?"

She always had an answer. I knew I could never beat her in a battle of logic. But she still hadn't offered me any support.

"Don't take it personally. We've both got our jobs to do," she said.

"So what help *can* you give us?" I asked.

Her eyes darted from left to right, to the screen of her computer and finally down to the floor. That one throwaway line had caught her off guard.

"Let's talk about it," she said weakly. "Have you discussed the figures with Larry Farlow?"

I told her I had, but I wanted her to see them as well.

"Well, I suppose you had better carry on along the lines you suggest. Get Farlow to run an opportunity workshop or whatever you call it, and let me know if anything useful comes out of it. Meanwhile, leave a copy of the risk register with me. I can at least check the sums."

If that was her idea of senior management support, heaven help us. There was no point in wasting my breath telling her that Jill, who had first-class honours in maths, had already double-checked the calculations. In any case, Jean had turned back to her spreadsheet.

"If you don't mind me saying so," I said, pointing at the screen, "there's something very odd about those figures." (Not that her spreadsheet meant a thing to me – it was just a stab in the dark.)

"Yes," she replied. "It's been bothering me, too. I'm not sure, but it might even be a bug in the software. I'll sort it out, though. Even if I have to stay here all night."

"I hope so," I said, the ambiguity intentional, and set off to find Larry and finalise the arrangements for Monday morning's session with the team.

The day began warm and bright, with a fine mist thinning quickly to leave a clear blue sky and just the gentlest of breezes. It was going to be a scorcher.

We had booked a meeting room in the Cliff Hotel, which overlooked a sandy cove; and, with the prospect of a celebratory dip once the workshop session was over, we had all brought our swimming gear.

"Let's begin with a Monday morning story," Larry said.

"I told you he's a nut case," Pete whispered.

Larry grinned. "Glad to meet someone else who's telepathic," he said. "That's precisely what this story is about."

He asked if any of us had ever had trouble getting walnuts out of their shells without breaking the kernels into tiny pieces. We had all come across the problem. Occasionally they come out cleanly, but all too often even when you smash them into little bits you still can't separate shell from nut. Pete said that he had thrown away most of the walnuts he had bought the previous Christmas because they had given him even more stress than he got during bid work.

"OK," Larry said. "Buying walnuts is risky. You never know how many are going to refuse to release their kernels. Well, once upon a time there was a company who made their living by packaging and selling walnut halves. They wanted to get rid of this risk, and so they held a brainstorming session. They considered lots of different ways of cracking nuts – in effect they were trying to improve the design of nutcrackers, albeit industrial ones. Then somebody said: *'If only we had a little man inside each nut. He could push from the inside and help separate the kernel from the shell.'*

"What do you think?" Larry asked.

"I suppose it could work," Jill said. "If you could find someone small enough."

"Good," Larry said. "It's vital to keep saying that sort of thing. *That could work if* ... Far more constructive than *Yes but* ..."

'That could work if ...' is far more constructive than 'Yes but ...'

Jill looked pleased with herself. "Did they find one?" she asked.

"Yes. Sort of," Larry said. "Pushing from the inside was the answer." And then he told us about the solution that was eventually adopted. Moisture is impressed into the nuts in a pressure chamber. When the pressure is suddenly released, the moisture turns to water vapour, expanding rapidly and pushing the shells away from the kernels. Every nut opens cleanly and the kernels can be easily sorted from the shells.

Then it was time to start working on real opportunities for the Bilston contract. We began with Larry reminding us of the four types of opportunities. He wrote the headings on a flipchart page and stuck them up on the wall:

> ◆ Copycat opportunities
> ◆ Windfalls
> ◆ Hidden opportunities
> ◆ Imagineered opportunities

"OK," he said. "Let's be copycats. What are the questions that could help us find copycat opportunities?"

We were slow getting started, but soon the list began to grow:

- ◆ Whom should we copy?
- ◆ Who else has done a job like this before?
- ◆ What parts of the job have we done before?
- ◆ What other market areas might have useful parallels with our own?

We found no definite opportunities, but we made an action list for investigating some of the more interesting possibilities. Here are just three of the ideas we came up with:

- ◆ Dave: do a search of contracts won by other Amsys divisions in recent years and get in touch with anyone with experience of installations which had to operate over wide temperature extremes.
- ◆ Nadia: see what she could find on the Internet that might help us with the matters of transporting the finished equipment and disposing of the obsolete kit.
- ◆ Jill: arrange to visit the university and see whether they were doing any research that could help us on those technical aspects of the job that were new to us.

Next we considered where, when and how we might expect to find windfall opportunities.

"What would you really like to have?" Larry asked. "Make a wish list and let's see if we can make some of them come true."

We came up with quite a list:

- ◆ A closer working relationship with Bilstons. They seem a very insular lot, and it would probably be easier to understand their requirements if we could meet informally once in a while.
- ◆ Confidence that we can get everything shipped to Delvington without damage. Some of the instrumentation is very sensitive and we might lose time in recalibrating it once the installation is complete.
- ◆ An alternative supplier for the special bearing system. RTW products are excellent, but they're not cheap and RTW always take months to produce what we want.
- ◆ A way of cutting the transportation costs. All the quotations received so far seem very expensive.

For those opportunities where we thought time or cost savings might be possible we had a guess at what would be realistic targets. Larry suggested that we should play safe and not be too ambitious in setting our targets at this stage. Even so, we ended up with enough ideas to give us confidence that we could shave at least another two weeks off the programme. That would bring us to within five weeks of Bilstons' required completion date.

I thought perhaps we ought to spend the last hour and a half before lunch having a look for hidden opportunities. Larry suggested we limit it to twenty minutes because he had something else planned.

"OK, so what's your biggest worry in this whole programme?" Larry asked.

"Overrunning," Jill said, and we all agreed that meeting the schedule was going to be very difficult.

"Right. Then what should we be looking out for?" Larry asked.

"Ways of saving time," I said immediately.

"There's not enough time to do the job properly," Dave said. "So what are we going to do about it?"

"When the work won't fit the time available it's better to ask *'What are we not going to do about it?'*" Larry corrected.

When the work won't fit the time available, ask 'What are we *not* going to do about it?'

He said that right now it seemed as if everything we had planned to do needed to be done, but if we took the right initiatives at the right time we ought to be able to make some of the work unnecessary.

We all liked the sound of that and asked where in the plan we should look for such opportunities.

"Mainly in the high-risk areas," Larry said. And so we went through the risk register highlighting the nature of the opportunities we intended to look for in each case.

The first of these was in understanding the customer's true requirements and priorities. We had already assumed in our risk assessment that this global risk area was significant. Experience told me that it is impossible to tie down a contract so fully that misunderstanding cannot occur. I also knew that few customers had a perfect understanding of what they wanted until they saw what you delivered. Then those apparently little changes that carry surprisingly big costs and cause schedule chaos can creep in and upset the best of plans.

We had an idea that we might be able to get much closer to our customer, to investigate the fine details of their real requirements with them, and to get any contract changes agreed early on when they would cost us very little but be of great value to Bilstons. And the opportunity we came up with to achieve all this was a two-way staff secondment, or possibly a short-term exchange. In theory it would cost each party next to nothing, and we ought to be able to save quite a lot of time – at least a fortnight, we felt – on the start-up phase.

Jill said it would be wise to sound out Bilstons on the idea before submitting our bid next week; I phoned, and they agreed to set up a meeting the next day to discuss the suggestion.

When we looked at the risks on long-delivery items of equipment, Jill had a couple of ideas. There wasn't time to go into detail, so we had to leave the rest of the opportunity log blank. Larry said that it was quite normal at this stage, and new opportunities were bound to emerge as we became more familiar with the job – as long as we looked for them.

"Right then," Larry said. "Who's for a swim before lunch? Nothing like a bit of exercise and a good lunch to put us in the right frame of mind for a spot of imagineering later on this afternoon."

And we went and built our raft.

It was great to see everybody having a good time, especially after the late evenings and lost weekends we had been through over the past few weeks.

"Can't be bad, can it?" Pete yelled as we ran down the beach and hurled ourselves into the surf. "Just think. We're getting paid for this! I wonder what old Gilbert would say if he knew."

Old he might be, but Gilbert Manning's heart was in the right place. I was sure he would have said something like 'Get on and enjoy yourselves. You deserve it.' But I couldn't help wondering what Jean Cartwright would make of Larry's opportunity workshop.

After lunch we sat and chatted awhile and then took a stroll along the sea shore. There was no sense of urgency about Larry Farlow, and yet he got results. And somehow we all knew instinctively when it was time to go back indoors and have a go at creating opportunities.

Back at our meeting room, we saw that tables had been put in a row along one wall. On the tables was a pile of newspapers and five pairs of scissors.

"Right, Jill," Larry said. "You're Industry. You take Education and Training, Dave. Pete – Environment Matters. Nadia – Social Events, Charities and the like. And you had better go for anything else that looks in the least bit interesting, Jim."

We all stood there, totally confused. Then I picked up one of the newspapers, *The Delvington and Mittlesham Gazette*, and suddenly the penny dropped.

"You want us to cut out news items in our various categories. Is that it?" I asked.

Larry nodded, unable to suppress a grin.

"OK, but why?" Dave asked. "What do we do then?"

"You decide!" Larry said, still smiling. "You're a creative team. I'm sure you can find a use for them. The biggest barrier to creativity is the mythical belief that you're simply not creative."

The biggest barrier to creativity is the belief that you are not creative

"Another obstacle you have to overcome is the concern that you don't know *how* to be creative. As far as I'm concerned, any way will do."

Another obstacle you must overcome is the concern that you don't know *how* to be creative

"So are newspaper cuttings a tried and tested way of bringing out creative ideas?" I asked.

"I'll explain later," Larry said. "We need to get started."

"Yes. Let's give it a go," Pete said, and we all got busy with our cuttings.

Pete said that he was organising his cuttings by date order.

"Good idea," Nadia said. "Let's all organise our cuttings in different ways. I'll try by numbers of people actually involved."

We all chose different ways of categorising our clippings. It took about half an hour and the floor was a mess when we had finished.

"Anybody spotted anything we might be able to use?" Larry asked.

Dave had found something interesting. "They're setting up a new telecommunications laboratory at Delvington College," he said. "It's due to open about the time we will be commissioning the new transmitter. I wonder if we could link the two events in some way."

"Yes," Nadia said. "And Bilstons will need some positive public relations exposure. They will be increasing the height of their transmitter mast, and it's hardly the prettiest of objects to grace the landscape."

"I wonder whether the college would be interested in fitting an antenna of their own to the mast." I mused. "Perhaps they would be keen to carry out experiments using microwave links of some sort."

"Wait a minute," Pete said. "Just supposing we got the college to take over the *old* mast site. It would save us the cost of dismantling the thing, and that far exceeds its scrap value."

"Yes, and I wonder if we could get Bilstons to sell them the old antenna facility," Dave said. "It's only an empty hut and a tatty old antenna mast on a tiny patch of derelict land. In years to come that old hut could become a liability, especially if kids break into it and have an accident there. I'll bet that's why Bilstons are insisting on us dismantling the old mast. Maybe they would consider giving it to the college. Or at least letting them have it on indefinite loan."

Talking over the idea, we soon realised that there were lots of potential opportunities of this type, both in our day-to-day business and in the special assignments and projects we had to manage. Just because something is of no use to you doesn't mean it has no value.

Just because something is of no use to you doesn't mean it has no value

Jill quoted a good example. Traditionally, people who produced fence posts had to bear the cost of removing the bark so that they could treat the timber with preservative. Nowadays the bark is chopped up, bagged and sold as mulch to restrict weed growth in shrubberies, borders and the like. A biodegradable product that needs periodic replacement. What could be better?

This set Nadia off on her hobby horse: environmental protection. She said that disposing of old vehicle tyres has been a problem for years, but nowadays the rubber can be stripped from the casing and turned into flexible chippings to go beneath playground equipment. This gives the twin benefits of improved safety in children's playgrounds and reduced environmental pollution.

Then the discussion turned to widening the use of information. We wondered if there were opportunities for sharing the findings of investigations, learning points and ideas for managing risks; and, of course, for finding and creating opportunities. Maybe we had access to information that was of little use to us but could be invaluable to Bilstons. Nadia suggested we could ask them, and maybe we should let them know what sort of information we would like them to look out for that could help us.

We agreed to consider the subject of creative reuse of materials, other resources and information in all of our opportunity reviews.

Another area we looked into was making things really easy and so reducing the time it takes people to learn how to do things – operating a piece of equipment, finding information, that sort of thing.

In our original plan for the Bilston contract we had included a three-week training programme for the operators and maintenance staff. Pete said that the estimate was based on experience of training users and maintainers of similar systems, but if we could make some of the training unnecessary we could possibly save a week or so.

One idea was to provide an interactive demonstration and training disk well in advance of the training course, so that the basic familiarisation training, which usually takes a couple of days, would be unnecessary. I wondered whether this might also become a useful promotional aid, showing potential customers just how easy our systems are to set up, use and maintain. We were developing something for our Web site in any case, so I made a note to get in touch with the people who were designing the Web pages and see if there were opportunities to deliver increased benefits at no additional cost.

Larry said that looking for opportunities for exploiting the potential synergy between work going on in different parts of the company was always worth doing. There might also be synergy between what Amsys is doing and what some of its customers or its key suppliers are doing. And there was an additional advantage in seeking these kinds of opportunities: you maintain closer links, and so communication becomes more proactive. The benefit of this is that people exchange information at a time when it is of maximum value rather than waiting until lack of information becomes apparent because of the problems it causes.

We cut costs in the most surprising areas. Nadia, who would be responsible for getting everything to the site, was concerned at the high cost of shipping materials to Delvington and holding them in secure warehousing. By constructing the antenna base first, we would be able to store a lot of our high-value tools and materials there, and this nearly halved our estimated ware-housing costs.

That was when Jill pointed out that Envirocycle had won a contract to build a big recycling plant in Delvington just under a year ago.

"They've just taken over one of the units on the new industrial estate half a mile away from us," Jill said. "I wonder whether we could team up with them to cut our shipment costs. The timing ought to be about right, so it's worth a try."

"Right. Perhaps looking for economies of scale could become one of our general strategies for maximising synergy," I said.

At the end of our first session, we had listed getting on for a dozen general strategies for opportunity hunting and produced five specific ideas which we felt confident we could exploit on the Bilston job.

Over tea, I asked Larry about the newspaper cuttings idea. Was it one of a number of tried and tested methods?

"It is now," he said. "I made it up two days ago. This was its trial run. I think I'll use it again when you and I get together with the divisional directors, but I wouldn't want to use the same idea every time."

"Why not, if it works?" I asked.

"It helps if you keep changing the methods you use," he replied. "You don't want to get stuck with a routine when looking for opportunities. Inventing a new process is motivating in itself, and you have the added advantage of the unpredictability of what will happen. Unpredictability may be a problem for logical systems but it is a distinct advantage in creative processes."

Unpredictability – a problem for logical systems – can be a distinct advantage in creative processes

Everyone agreed that the workshop had been a great success, and we worked well into the evening to put all the new figures into the plan.

By lunch-time the next day we had everything we needed for Jean's meeting with the chief executive.

It took me an age to get to sleep that night. Sleepless nights were nothing new to me, but usually it was worry that kept me awake. This was different. Now my head was buzzing with the excitement of our achievements. I could hardly wait to get on with the job of putting the ideas into practice. Now I knew we were going to win the order *and* meet our promises to Bilstons. And we would make a respectable profit on the contract.

"Yes, that's quite true, Mr Manning, it is a high-risk job," Jean was saying as I was ushered in to the chief executive's office, "so I've asked Jim Hallam to join us. In case you need to go into any of the details."

"No, no. That's not what this meeting is for," the chief executive said firmly. He turned to me. "Hello, Jim. Take a seat. Jean tells me you and your team have been to hell and back to get this bid ready in time. Thanks for that. I'll be over to see the team later this afternoon. The least I can do is to thank them personally."

Superficially, Gilbert Manning was an unimposing figure. But he was an impressive person once you got to know him. His hunched, rather untidy appearance concealed a thoughtful, tough but caring man with a clear sense of priorities. He would not hesitate to close a division of Amsys if it was the right thing to do, but he always took a very personal interest in the people who were affected by his decisions. My dealings with him had been limited to the occasional meeting when Jean or her predecessor had been away on holiday. I liked him, but I wasn't at all sure what he thought of me and my team. We were very small cogs in his machine.

"Thanks, Gilbert," I said. "I won't pretend it's been easy. But we have had a lot of help."

The chief executive beamed at Jean, who didn't so much as bat an eyelid.

"Larry Farlow, from Transport, has been helping Jim quite a lot," Jean said quickly.

"Yes, I know. The opportunity-management man," the chief executive said. "I've seen some of his ideas. And so have you, Jean. Intriguing, don't you think? We need to get the whole of the organisation thinking that way." He turned to me: "I'm glad that you and your people have taken to Larry's ideas, Jim. How useful have they been?"

I explained how we had made a plan that had brought our forecast schedule down to eighty-one weeks. I said that the whole team was now committed to the concept of opportunity management and that in our workshop with Larry we had found a dozen opportunities that we intended to exploit in the early stages of the contract. There would be a series of opportunity review meetings, I told him, and I said that I was confident we would find the extra three weeks of schedule saving that we needed.

Jean stepped forward.

"I'm sorry, Gilbert," she said. "I've been through the figures and I can't fault them. This really is the best we can do."

Gilbert Manning frowned. "Jim says we can do the job, we can find the savings necessary to meet the schedule Bilstons are asking for, and we can make a decent profit on the deal, probably winning some more profitable orders from Bilstons while we're at it. What's your problem, Jean?"

"Er, I thought you would want to know exactly *how* we are going to solve all the problems," she said, "but we don't know."

"*Yet*," Gilbert added. He shook his head. "You don't know yet, and I wouldn't expect you to. In fact if you did I would be extremely nervous, because it would mean your approach was not an innovative one and we would almost certainly be heading for failure with our bid. Larry Farlow will explain what I mean when we have our next workshop with the rest of the divvies."

Turning to me he said: "You'll be there, won't you, Jim? I understand you are going to enlighten us on the work you and your team have done in putting this bid together. We'll also be keen to hear how the job itself is going, of course. You'll be working on the contract by then, if Bilstons keep to their own schedule."

"That's right," I told him.

He turned back to Jean.

"Right now, all that you and I need to know is that we have a team who will be able to solve the many problems that are bound to crop up along the way. This plan is a very convincing demonstration that you have built such a team. Well done, Jean. We'll also need your expert analytical skills when we're monitoring the job and reporting progress to Bilstons. We'll need to get that right. They are rather good at nit-picking, I'm told."

Neither Jean nor I missed the twinkle in his eye. If there was a problem – commercial, technical or interpersonal – anywhere in the organisation you could bet your socks the old man knew about it. He was well aware of the growing pains Jean was suffering. I, too, began to feel a little sympathy for her. Nobody was interested in her spreadsheets at this stage. But there was also a message there for me: I needed to appreciate that she had something of value to offer the team. The important thing was to learn to recognise when I needed Larry's brand of imaginative thinking and when I needed Jean's analytical, thorough style.

The chief then asked me what our overall strategy was, and I was ready for that one.

"First, I want to move to the position where we have two or three weeks in hand. Thereafter, our main focus will be on finding and creating opportunities for cutting costs and perhaps being able to offer Bilstons some extra benefits. We need the work, so it would also be good to extend the scope of the contract. By the time we are six months into this job I want us to have found and capitalised on all the schedule savings we need and to be managing the contract to maximise our profitability and the follow-on order potential."

The chief executive stared at the approval sheet for a few moments. And then he signed it.

"I wish all my decisions were as easy as this. With such a clear vision of how you intend running this job, I'm sure you and your team will do us proud. It's a good proposal and a very competitive bid. Let's go with it."

He handed the authorised form to Jean. "You've got some really good people, Jean. Look after them for us," he said.

I could see that she was struggling to think of something constructive to say. To her credit, though, she nodded and gave me an encouraging smile.

"Oh, and one last thing, both of you. I am expecting you to organise something a bit special to celebrate our winning this contract. Keep me informed, won't you?"

We submitted the Bilston bid on time and everyone breathed sighs of relief, thinking that for a while at least we could look forward to weekends off. But the relief was short-lived: the next two months were almost as hectic as the bidding phase. It was as if our proposal had spurred Bilstons to think about what they *really* wanted. Three new versions of the requirements document appeared in rapid succession, and we were kept busy late into the evenings refining our approach, replanning, re-estimating, rewriting the proposal, reassessing the risks and looking for new opportunities. Then suddenly it was all over: we had won.

The team members were jubilant; the chief exec was ecstatic. Even Jean managed a smile when she dropped in for half an hour to our celebration barbecue.

Although winning the Bilston contract had been heralded as a great success throughout the organisation, any relief that our jobs were safe for the time being was tinged with anxiety at the toughness of the targets we had to meet. The cost-saving opportunities we had committed ourselves to had enabled us to quote a competitive price, but we had also promised to deliver in seventy-eight weeks even though our best estimate was that the work would take eighty-one. Three weeks is still a lot to save on an eighteen-month programme – in an organisation prone to slipping on its schedules and delivering late.

With Larry's help we had been able to put together a credible baseline plan, and into this we had built a range of risk-mitigation counter-measures. Reactive contingency plans were also in place to help us deal with any remaining problems that might arise. And we had an opportunity-management plan.

We were very well off for plans.

What we were less well off for was experience in actually using plans to make management decisions as work proceeds. In the past it would have been a case of follow the project plan until we come up against the first impassable obstacle and then fall back into traditional crisis management – trying out all sorts of things in no particular order until we found a way through or around the impasse. By that time, of course, the original work schedule would be just about meaningless and we would have to replan the remainder of the work with new milestone dates and, invariably, a reduced profit forecast. Then some hapless soul – usually me – would have the unenviable task of breaking the news to our customer that we would be late in completing the job. This process was sometimes repeated two or three times before the contract shuddered to a close and everyone, the customer included, breathed a sigh of relief and vowed 'never again'.

We were all looking forward to seeing what difference harnessing the unicorn of opportunity would make.

Larry had said that reviewing the risks and our plans for managing them would be essential and that we would need to include risk reviews in our progress meetings and, if necessary, in the technical updates, too. Compared with our previous method of working, the difference this made was remarkable. Instead of waiting for something to go wrong, we discussed each of the risks in turn and either took avoiding action or introduced counter-measures to reduce the impact and probability of problems. Proactive management became a way of life. As work proceeded we found that we were able to describe many of the risks more clearly. This made it easier to forecast and be on the lookout for symptoms indicating that things were beginning to go wrong. No problem ever received a warm welcome, but we all knew that by discovering problems earlier more options would be available for dealing with them.

If you discover problems earlier, you generally have more options for dealing with them

In effect, by our counter-measures activities we had built increased flexibility into our plan, and so we had fewer crises. We had also budgeted for the crises, so we could move into action right away and activate the contingency plans.

For example, when we made our initial risk-management plan we identified the cooling system as a possible risk area. Pete felt that there might be problems, but he had very little idea what they might be and so the description was rather vague.

Risk Area: *The transmitter cooling system might be a problem because the equipment has to work in such a harsh environment.*

Very early on we settled for a pressurised heat exchanger, having carried out detailed calculations on the performance of a simple air-cooled system and shown that it would not be adequate. Cost-wise there was little to choose between the alternatives but the risks were very different in each case, and so we had to amend the risk-management plan to take account of this change. Still six months before we had any heat exchangers to test, we were able to improve our proactive risk-management plan and to refine the estimates for reactive risk management if things did go wrong in the testing.

Risk Area: *The transmitter cooling system might be a problem because the equipment has to work in a harsh environment.*

Risk: *The transmitter might overheat. The heat exchanger will need to be tested to check whether it can operate safely at the high ambient temperatures encountered at Delvington, and if the prototype fails these tests we will have to modify it and redo all the tests. The extra cost and delay would be very serious.*

A couple of months later, and still twelve weeks before the transmitter testing was due to begin, it became clear that we would have to pressure-test the whole cooling system. This was something else we had not bargained for. Fortunately, we had time to assess the options of subcontracting the work or doing it ourselves and maybe even setting up our own test facility. Unsurprisingly, subcontracting turned out to be less costly than setting up our own facility, but at this stage something very useful came out of one of our opportunity-management sessions and it changed the situation dramatically.

Larry attended the risk-review meeting at which Pete reported that Bilstons were very worried about the safety hazard associated with a pressurised cooling system. Not only would we need to test the system at its normal working pressure, but we would also have to show that every cooling element was capable of withstanding pressures well above its normal operating range. Alternatively we would need to carry out destructive pressure testing on one of the cooling systems to demonstrate what the actual safety margin was; this, the experts agreed, was the most cost-effective approach in the long run. We hadn't anticipated needing to do any of this, of course. It wasn't in our baseline plan and there was no contingency plan for dealing with the extra work involved, which represented a serious threat to our delivery schedule (not to mention a substantial bill for which we had no budget).

"Our plan is a failure, Larry," Pete said. "It doesn't solve all of our problems. We're back into crisis mode again."

"I wouldn't say that," Larry replied. "Not yet, at least. You've merely reached a point where you have an unexpected turn of events. That happens in most jobs, unless they are so trivial that they can manage themselves. In which case, you would all be out of a job. This kind of situation is one of the main reasons for your existence as a team. View it as a challenge, certainly, but when you get an unexpected outcome don't automatically treat it as failure.

An unexpected outcome is not necessarily a failure

"The worst that could happen is that you have to plan now for a crisis in the offing. But at the moment it's only a potential problem, a risk that might even contain hidden opportunities."

Opportunities may be hidden within the risks represented by an unexpected outcome

I had learnt that when things go awry it's usually unwise to continue working to the original plan, but this sounded like Larry saying 'Forget the goal and set a new one.' I asked him if this was what he intended.

"Certainly not. You have to achieve what you promised Bilstons you would achieve. It's just that you need to find a way of doing it without jeopardising any of your other promises. The completion date is vital to Bilstons; the profit margin to Amsys. Look at the situation from other perspectives. How could this unexpected outcome be good news rather than bad? What would have to be different?"

When the unexpected happens, ask 'What would have to change for this to be good news?'

"Search me." Nadia and Pete said in synchronism, and I could see that Jill was lost, too. Larry was really trying to tell us that it was time to make use of our creativity and to look for the opportunities that this risk might contain.

I recalled the advice he had given me some months earlier, when I had dived straight into an attempted creative workshop without some kind of warm-up exercise or an example of how other people had turned an unexpected outcome to their advantage. Larry's opportunity notebook lay on the table before him, and I seized the opportunity.

"Somewhere in there," I said, pointing at the battered old logbook, "there must be an example of how someone else turned a sticky situation such as ours into an opportunity. Remind us how it's done, Larry."

Larry thumbed the dog-eared pages, grinning broadly and muttering: "Sticky situations – ah, yes. Here we are . . ."

He closed the logbook. I don't know whether he had looked up a relevant case study or whether it had all been for theatrical effect, but he had our undivided attention.

"Adhesives are for sticking," he said, "and the more firmly they stick the better. For most purposes, that is. But one innovative product would never have seen the light of day if the 3M Company had closed their minds to the value of an adhesive that does *not* stick too well. What 3M did was to turn the risk of failure – that the adhesive might peel off rather than sticking permanently – into a certainty. The result is history, so to speak. They used an *unsuccessful* adhesive to produce their Post-It® Notes. These ubiquitous little message notes can always be removed and replaced elsewhere. As an adhesive 'failure' the Post-It® idea has been incredibly successful.

"That's right," Nadia said. "Everybody uses them. I wish we could have good ideas like that."

"OK, so how are we going to handle this problem creatively?" I asked the team. "If we can be creative it needn't be a setback at all."

There were one or two useful suggestions for rescheduling various aspects of the work to offset the inevitable delay while the pressure testing was being arranged. We even looked at the possibility of cutting back on other parts of the test programme, but my intuition told me that we would live to regret such a decision. The biggest risk, in terms of impact, was that the pressurised coolant tank might fracture during test: for safety, we needed to subject it to three times its normal working pressure. If the tank fractured we would have to modify it and then repeat the tests, and this would take at least another month – maybe even six weeks.

"To avoid the risk of missing the deadline, we really need to do the tests in the next couple of months," Larry said. "Have you got a tank that could be tested?"

"Well, yes," Pete said. "But there's no way we could build a test facility in that time. That's a hell of a lot of work. In any case, it would take at least eight weeks to get the necessary test equipment ordered and delivered. And if we want to use a specialist test house, which is the only other alternative, we will have to take our place in the queue. You can't just walk in and demand immediate attention, you know. They're booked up solid for months in advance. I don't mean to be negative, but let's face it, Larry. We're in a hole and our carefully thought-out risk-management plan isn't going to get us out."

"I agree," Larry replied. "So we need to change the plan. Maybe we should jump the queue for testing. And we also need to save money. So while we're at it, why don't we try to get one of these specialist test houses to do the work at cost. Or maybe even free of charge? That way, we get back on schedule and avoid busting the budget."

"These test house people aren't stupid, you know," Pete said. "You can't expect them to . . ."

"Wait a minute," Jill interrupted. "You mean maybe there's an opportunity here. Is that it?"

"Most likely," Larry replied. "The challenge is to find it. Or to create it."

"OK," Jill said. "So we need to say things beginning with *'That could work if . . .'* rather than *'That won't work because . . .'* "

And that is what we did. All sorts of crazy ideas came out of our brainstorming session, and I'm prepared to bet that we could have got the testing completed on schedule at little or no cost to us in a whole lot of ways. The idea we settled for came from Nadia, the most junior member of the team. She told us that at the weekend she had watched a movie in which a factory chimney collapsed during a storm, flattening the baddies just as they were about to mow down the good guys.

"It must be pretty serious when one of these tanks explodes," she said. "Why don't we team up with someone who specialises in safety training? This would be a brilliant introduction to a safety training film. It would also be excellent, low-cost publicity for the test house. And maybe we could recover some of *our* costs, too."

"Why not? Let's give it a try," Jill said, and we all agreed.

"I happen to be on pretty good terms with Val Tarrant. She's a director of SMT, one of the best safety training companies in the business," Pete said. "Val and I went to college together. I'll see if I can interest her in the idea, but I'll say that it has got to be during the next eight weeks or never. SMT will soon realise that if they turn down this opportunity we're likely to approach one of their rivals."

"That's great," Jill said. "I'm sure any of the top-flight test houses would want to be in on the publicity."

The deal took a bit of setting up, but we managed it with a fortnight to spare. The test facility didn't cost us a bean, and the tank withstood nearly four times its maximum working pressure before the big bang. We got to see the action, which was filmed from five different angles, to be played back in slow motion. Bathed in multi-colour laser light, the explosion was spectacular. Coolant sprayed out like an articulated rainbow and chunks of casing flew through the air.

Three months later the safety training company sent us a complimentary copy of their training film. We had loaned them an early mock-up of the complete cooling system, and so the film they made was highly realistic. Three workers had just left the building when the tank blew up: the place was completely gutted, and so in the film it appeared as if the workers had narrowly escaped being blown to smithereens. I had a sneaking suspicion that they would make more money out of it than we would out of our contract with Bilstons. But who cares? We got the opportunity we wanted, and the test house was featured in the training programmes of many of its potential customers. Bilstons were delighted, too: despite the initial setback, the testing phase had been completed on schedule.

When I showed Larry the footage of the exploding tank his only comment was: "Wow! Some unicorn!"

The other opportunities we found and created were nowhere near as way out as that one, but together they all provided vital cost and time savings. For example, in another division of the organisation we found there was a product development going on that needed special components very similar to some we were designing into the Bilston job. They needed ten times as many as we had expected to use, and by working together we were able to incorporate suitable fixings and features to make the same part do both jobs. That saved us a fortune in tooling and set-up costs. On another occasion we loaned an unfinished unit to Bilstons so that they could take a set of photographs in preparation for a product launch, and at the same time they got their photographer to do some internal shots for our new capability brochure. We made their life easier, and they saved us money.

Sometimes it was the other way round, with our suppliers benefiting from something that we were doing with things they had shipped to us. Gradually, it became a habit to look for these sorts of opportunities. It meant keeping in touch with our customer and our suppliers, but, surprisingly perhaps, this didn't take up much time: we became more efficient communicators as well as more effective in communicating at the right time. Mostly this involved letting people know well in advance what we were doing for them or what we needed from them. A great many of these opportunities just seemed to get swept out from little corners, but others we had to go in search of.

The real payoff from all this came from the really close working relationships we forged with our key suppliers: when we needed them to do something special to help us out of a tricky situation, they really did pull out all the stops. It was a win–win deal: both parties did much more asking for help *before* things went wrong, and as a result a lot less time was spent on fire-fighting.

Don't get me wrong: there were still plenty of problems. We would never have succeeded on the Bilston project without good crisis management. But, by using our risk-management plan as a prompt for timely decision making, we had fewer crises and more time to consider the options for dealing with them. Larry called this a move from disorganised chaos to organised crisis management. Maybe he was right, but the panic level was greatly reduced.

As we approached an identified high-risk point, we put a lot more effort into monitoring. We had a reasonable idea of the symptoms that would indicate a problem in the offing, and at the first sign of things going awry I called the key people together to review the contingency plan. Quite often we could see new options that none of us had thought of when we made the original plan, and this gave us the opportunity to reduce the effect on our schedule and budget when a risk did become reality. Some risks we avoided altogether. For many others we were able to mitigate the effects by low-cost counter-measures, not all of which were the original ideas we had thought of when we first drew up the risk register. More importantly, as our vision of the later stages of the job became clearer, when we reviewed the risks that we had anticipated meeting towards the end of the programme we were often able to substitute a low-cost counter-measures initiative for a more costly (reactive) contingency plan. As a result, we were able to save two weeks on the schedule. (In effect, we had been able to reduce the exposure to schedule risk by two weeks.) This meant that our opportunity-management target could now be reduced: we had to find opportunities amounting to a further schedule saving of just one week. After that, any additional savings we found would be a safety margin against the unforeseen – not forgetting that built into the contract there was a small but worthwhile incentive for early completion.

There was one point when things began to look very serious and team morale plummeted. Everything had seemed to be going well. We were becoming increasingly professional in our teamwork, reviewing the creative and analytical processes we used and setting improvement targets, as good teams do. And then, right out of the blue, disaster. A consignment of essential supplies got lost in transit. Irretrievably lost.

"Without the transmitter modules I can't do a thing," Pete said. "Insurance will cover the financial loss, but we'll have to delay all work on the transmitter until we get replacement modules. Needless to say, they're not standard items. They have to be built to our specification."

"Are the suppliers pulling out all the stops to help us?" I asked.

Pete said that they were. Normally it took months to get custom modules built, but our suppliers had rescheduled their other workload and put us right at the head of the queue. The replacement modules would be with us in three to four weeks: it took that long to get everything through the manufacturing processes. We simply had to sweat it out.

The trouble was, Bilstons wanted to use one of our sub-systems for some interoperability trials – and they were working from our plan, which said the sub-system would be available in plenty of time. Now we were going to have to let them down.

We told Jean about the problem, and without a moment's hesitation she called Larry in. She wanted his opinion on the best thing to do in the circumstances.

Larry seemed reluctant to give us any direct advice. "Well, someone, somewhere, has made a mistake," he said. "What does your customer think about it?" he asked.

"He doesn't know, but I can guess what he will say when he finds out," I replied. "I thought it best to try everything we could before telling him. After all, we're being paid to do the worrying for him, aren't we?"

Larry grimaced. "Hm, my guess may be rather different from yours," he said. "I would think he'll say something like *'Why the hell didn't somebody tell me about this sooner?'* Don't you think so?"

He was right. I nodded.

"As far as Bilstons are concerned," Larry continued, "I'm sure they would prefer a high-profile problem rather than damage out of sight, below the water line."

A high-profile problem is preferable to damage hidden below the water line

"We all make mistakes. Nobody's perfect," Jill added.

Pete was showing signs of frustration: he was staring resolutely out of the window to avoid Larry's gaze.

"What's the matter, Pete?" Larry asked.

"Nothing. Well, it's just that what you are saying doesn't seem to stack up with our business policies."

"Such as?" Larry prompted.

"The *No Surprises* policy, for instance. And the *Right First Time* objective."

"Hm, I see what you mean," Larry said. "We certainly don't welcome nasty surprises, but hidden nasties are usually the most damaging. I'm not trying to undermine the objective of trying to get more of our work right first time. When we know what *is* right. But when you are doing innovative work you have to accept that you won't get everything right. The trick is to spot your mistakes early and put them right at a lower cost than your competitors could. But the only way you can hope to avoid making any mistakes is to play safe and avoid risk and innovation."

The only way to avoid making mistakes is to play safe and avoid risk and innovation

We all agreed that there was no future for Amsys without innovation.

"What really matters," Larry continued, "is how you behave when things do go wrong."

Pete turned to Larry and said: "I suppose in situations like this it all boils down to assessing your customer's priorities before you decide on your course of action."

"That's right," Larry agreed. "So in the particular case of these missing modules, what will be the effect on your customer's plans?"

We sat there in silence.

"Don't you *know*?" he persisted.

"I've got a hunch that he intends to use the prototype in a link-up with some other system that he has under development," I said. "Unfortunately I don't have the details."

"Well, who *has*?" Larry pressed.

"Only the people at Bilstons, I guess," I told him, "and maybe whoever is supplying the other sub-system. They probably know more than we do, because they are involved in the link testing."

"I think you're right, Larry," Jean said. "We need to find out. One of us" – she looked at me – "ought to give Bilstons a call."

I said I would get on to them right away.

"Good," Larry said. "But it's not a good idea to try and sort out this kind of problem over the phone. Arrange to go and see them. Or invite them here to see the situation first-hand and talk through the options for managing it."

"Managing the situation!" Nadia said. "You have a clever way with words, Larry Farlow."

"Managing a difficult situation so that it doesn't become an impossible one is being smart," he replied. "Merely worrying about it is no substitute."

Managing a difficult situation is smart; worrying about it is no substitute

I called John Mellor, our main contact at Bilstons, and gave him the news. He wasn't very pleased, but he said he was glad I had told him right away because he would have to reschedule the interoperability trials. We agreed to get together that afternoon, and it was just as well we did: when John learned that the problem was with the transmitter module his face lit up.

"No problem," he said. "We're only planning on testing the link in one direction at this stage. In two weeks' time we will need your sub-system to operate as a receiver. The transmitter won't be needed for at least another month, so if you can get the problem with the transmitter module sorted by then it won't affect our trials programme at all. Any chance you can manage that?"

I told him that we had two new transmitter modules coming in at the end of the month, and that would give us plenty of time to get everything tested and ready for the second phase of the interoperability trials. The other things John would require we could easily bring forward; we had everything to hand and it just meant some minor rescheduling.

The meeting began with us expecting to be given a difficult time, but it ended with John Mellor thanking us for rescheduling things to help him with his trials.

"We should have forewarned you about our intended trials," he said. "I'm sorry about the short notice. And thanks for taking the initiative to call this meeting. It has taken us barely an hour to sort things out, and we have avoided what might otherwise have become a lot of hassle later."

After that experience, I promised myself that never again would I keep a customer in the dark about a threat to a key delivery date. The episode had brought it home to me that with your customer as a member of your team it's amazing how much easier it is to solve, or find ways of getting around, problems before they arise.

With your customer as a member of your team, it is easier to solve problems before they arise

Before going home, I went to see Larry and told him how the matter had been resolved.

"I must admit, we were very lucky," I said. "Supposing their trials plan *hadn't* been phased so that Bilstons needed our receiver first. Then what would we have done?"

Larry was silent for a few moments. "I wonder whether you would have found *other* ways of being lucky," he said. "Maybe you would have worked out some sort of arrangement that was acceptable to your customer. Or maybe not. Maybe you would have missed the deadline and let your customer down and maybe he would have cancelled the whole contract and sued you for damages. We'll never know. But what we do know is that you would have managed the situation professionally. There is no guarantee of success, you know. Proactive risk and opportunity management pushes the odds in your favour, but sometimes Lady Luck turns her back on the best of managers. You must expect to have some setbacks. Nobody wins all of the time."

> **Sometimes Lady Luck turns her
> back on the best of managers;
> nobody should expect to win all
> of the time**

"And then what?"

"You have a painful but valuable opportunity to learn from the experience. Failure is not best forgotten. It is an opportunity that in many organisations gets thrown away."

> **Failures are not best forgotten.
> Remember – they are
> opportunities to learn**

"Why? I mean, what *should* happen?" I asked.

"In some cases perhaps the people involved in a failure are so embarrassed that they prefer to pretend nothing untoward has happened. It's understandable, perhaps, in organisations with a blame culture. You know – where whenever something goes obviously wrong everyone rushes around trying to find who was at fault and to prove that it certainly wasn't themselves. As for putting things right, that gets very low priority until the culprit, or should I say the scapegoat, has been duly humiliated. Well, you can just imagine how people's attitudes to learning opportunities are affected by that sort of treatment."

I recognised the kind of organisation Larry was describing. It wasn't so different from the way we were until very recently. '*I can prove it wasn't my fault*', and '*Don't blame me, I was only doing what I was told*', and '*I haven't had anything in writing yet so there's nothing I can do about it*' – these were the standard responses whenever the going got tough.

"Whether the Bilston job turns out well or not so well, you ought to hold a post-mortem to find out why," Larry urged.

Whether a job turns out well or not, hold a post-mortem to find out why

I could see some point of holding an investigation if things go badly. We need to know what caused the problems so that we can do better on future jobs. But why hold a post-mortem on a success story, I wondered?

Larry read my mind. "When things go exceptionally well, you do need to find out why. Only then can you decide whether it is reasonable to expect future work to go just as well."

When things go exceptionally well, you need to learn whether it is realistic to expect future work to go just as well

"You mean, did we benefit from an unusually large number of windfall opportunities? That sort of thing?" I asked.

"Yes, exactly. If you did, praise the team for having the foresight to be in the apple orchard at the right time, but recognise that the same apples can't fall from the tree more than once. Er, not unless you do something *exceptionally* creative to make it happen."

The same apples cannot fall from the tree more than once – unless you do something *exceptionally* creative

Larry laughed at my confusion. "It doesn't make much sense to me, either," he admitted. "It's just that I almost broke my golden rule of never saying 'never' or 'always'. It's a rule we should never break – well, hardly ever. But, to be serious, it is important to share what you learn – not only with your team members but also among other people in the organisation who can benefit from your experience. Take your opportunity-management plan, for instance. How will you maximise the benefit from your investment in that plan?"

"Well, it has already helped us on the work itself," I said. "Surely that's the payoff."

"That's the short-term payoff, certainly, and I'm really pleased that you are finding it a useful technique. But potentially there are longer-term benefits, too. For instance, by the end of this job you and your team should be pretty adept at recognising, tracking down and creating opportunities, and experienced in producing and using opportunity-management plans. That makes you a much more competent team."

"Right. I agree with that, Larry," I told him. "But a post-mortem won't alter that, so why waste the time and money?"

"Did you learn anything about the process of becoming competent at opportunity management?" Larry asked. "And knowing what you know now, are there any things that you would want to avoid? Or things you would tackle differently if you were starting the whole process again?"

"Oh, sure," I told him. "But the point is, we're not starting again, and . . ."

"*You're* not," Larry cut in. "But *others* might be. Other teams in your division or elsewhere in the organisation. Would you want them to make the mistakes you did? Or would you want this to be a learning organisation in which we share our experiences and so avoid unnecessary repetition of mistakes?"

I said I could see his point.

"And how about letting other people know how you achieved the breakthroughs that allowed you to save time on the job and meet a deadline that seemed almost impossible at the outset?" he asked. "The best way I know of doing this is to hold a post-mortem review and to circulate a brief report. And I do mean *brief*. Anything more than a couple of pages needs summarising again. Cover the really significant points, not everything, and invite those who would like more details to contact you.

"The most important part of any post-mortem review is the action plan," he said.

The most important part of any post-mortem review is the action plan

"Aim to get the actions cleared and the learning points shared within a month of the post-mortem, before the team members get too deeply immersed in their next jobs. That way, there is a much higher chance that what you have learned will get incorporated into the plans for future work."

There was no arguing with Larry's logic. Learning is only of value in business if you put it into practice.

Learning is only of value if you put it into practice

Looking back on it, the workshop Larry and I ran for the divisional directors was one of the most exciting (and mentally exhausting) days of my life. We had beaten the best in the world to win the Bilston contract, so everyone was really interested in my case-study presentation. I made the risk- and opportunity-management plan my main topic, because Bilstons had told us that it was this that had finally swung their decision in our favour.

I won't say that Jean Cartwright became a fervent Larry Farlow disciple overnight, but I've never seen anyone take so many notes at a seminar. She hogged question time, and even old Gilbert Manning, who topped and tailed each session with his own straight-to-the-point introductions and summaries, had difficulty getting a word in.

How did we do overall on the Bilston job?

Well, in the end we easily beat the schedule target *and* we made a very respectable profit on the contract. Bilstons received everything they were expecting, and the whole system was fully operational with two weeks to spare. It was a quality system, too, with remarkably few teething problems. Bilstons were very impressed. Within a year of us completing this job, Johnny

Mellor and his people awarded three more contracts to Amsys –
two of them considerably bigger than the Delvington job.

I learned a lot while working on that first Bilston contract, and I
recorded quite a few new learning points in my opportunity
notebook.

Subject: Getting results

- Estimating is based on hindsight; target setting requires foresight.
- Estimates presume we will perform as in the past; targets imply an intention to improve.
- 'That could work if . . .' is more constructive than 'Yes but . . .'
- When the work won't fit the time available, ask 'What are we *not* going to do about it?'
- The biggest barrier to creativity is the belief that you're not creative.
- Just because something is of no use to you doesn't mean it has no value.
- Unpredictability can be an advantage in a creative process.
- An unexpected outcome is not necessarily a failure.
- When the unexpected happens, ask 'What would have to change for this to be *good* news?'
- A high-profile problem is preferable to damage below the water line.
- Managing the situation is smart; worrying about it is no substitute.
- With your customer as a member of your team, it is easier to solve problems before they arise.
- Failures are *not* best forgotten. Remember – they are opportunities to learn.
- When things go exceptionally well, you need to learn whether it is realistic to expect future work to go just as well.
- The same apples cannot fall from the tree more than once – unless you do something *exceptionally* creative to make it happen.
- The most important part of any post-mortem review is the action plan.
- Learning is only of value if you put it into practice.

Action: I must continue to seize every opportunity to learn more about managing opportunity.

Chapter 8

Life, the unreversible – and everything

Three weeks after we completed the Bilston job, Larry Farlow left Amsys to head up an international aid organisation. As he said, if helping other people is what you really enjoy doing, why not make a career of it?

For Amsys, this was a serious loss, but one that Gilbert Manning had obviously foreseen. The Bilston contract was, I now realised, Gilbert's means of turning this risk into an opportunity, and he had made sure that the opportunity was managed well: he got Larry to manage it.

As we had got further into the work for Bilstons, Larry Farlow had gradually reduced his involvement in our day-to-day activities. He still sat in on the occasional session when we asked him to, but even then his role was more as an observer than as a facilitator. To a large extent we had become a self-facilitating team. Within a few months of winning the contract the original team of Jill, Dave, Nadia, Pete and I were fully sold on the concepts of opportunity management and we were pretty comfortable with the processes involved. Jill and I were also involved with other teams – not only in Comms division but in

Transport and Business Services, too – coaching them in the concepts and techniques; that was something old Gilbert Manning instigated, and Jean had been happy for us to continue in the role at least until we had trained our successors.

Personally, I had been keen to learn still more, and about once a month Larry and I had continued our discussions, either during lunch break or over a drink after work. By then I was doing more than asking questions and listening to the answers of the guru: I was making some useful contributions of my own. It was gratifying, on occasion, to find Larry Farlow asking for my opinions and recording them in his own opportunity notebook. We were learning together.

I'll always remember my last lunch-time chat with Larry. It was a week or so before I heard that he would be leaving. He asked me what at the time seemed a very odd sort of question: "If you could do anything you wanted, anything at all, what would you really like to be doing right now?"

"I don't honestly know, Larry," I told him. "I've never thought about it. I quite like the job I've got, especially now. Now that I feel equipped to cope with it. And now that I can spend some quality time with Mary and the twins."

"Good for you," he said. "But I do hope you're going to apply your new skills to managing yourself as well as to managing your work. Risk and opportunity are everywhere. There's no need to restrict the concept of opportunity management to your day job. Opportunity management is a life skill. You only live once. You can't go back and try again to get it right the second time – as far as I know. Think about it."

Life is a unique opportunity – as far as we know

I did. I still do. And the more I think about what Larry told me the more I come to appreciate its full significance. But at the time I was still a novice, so I asked if he knew of examples from the real world, not just from the world of work. I hoped that, with a few ideas just to get me started, I could organise my life a bit better. I wanted to be successful and *happy*. Who doesn't?

Larry told me a bit more about himself. Outside work he was an avid reader, and by all accounts he had a pretty impressive collection of books. Serious stuff, mostly – philosophy, the fundamental sciences and, not surprisingly, management theory. He told me he got through five or six books a month. (I might *start* two or three, but in those days I counted it a good month if I finished reading *one*.)

"Sounds like an expensive hobby," I said.

"It could be. But most of my books don't cost me a thing. As a matter of fact, I get paid for reading some of them."

"You're kidding!" I replied.

He wasn't. He told me that he was a book reviewer for *Management in Focus*, and that he also did a monthly books slot on our local radio station.

"Wait a minute – Lionel Whatsisname – "

Larry grinned. "Lionel Farringdon-Smythe. Delighted to be on the wireless and at your service," he said in a reedy, supercilious voice that I had come to associate with Sunday evenings on the radio.

"I might have guessed," I said. "So that's *your* nom de plume. Or should I say nom de *plum*? Well, I've got news for you, Larry. For the last two years I've been buying just about every management and philosophy book you've been recommending. And who knows? One day maybe I might even get round to reading them."

"You should have said something, Jim. You could have borrowed mine," Larry said. "Still, at least you've got the makings of a useful reference library."

"But – an international business magazine. How did you swing that one?"

"Well, not by sitting about at home – or at work for that matter – hoping that someone would telephone and ask me to be a book reviewer. I harnessed the unicorn, Jim," he said with an impish grin.

"Opportunity creation followed by opportunity management," I offered.

"Precisely!" Larry agreed. "Vision, plan, action."

Vision → plan → action
– the opportunity-management
process

"It really does work," he continued. "But not just for me. Did I ever tell you about Sally Cotterell?"

"No. What about her?"

"Well," Larry replied. "I first met Sally at one of her Creative Problem Solving courses. By the way, it's a really good course – have you been on it yet?" I shook my head, and Larry continued: "You ought to. Sally's a brilliant course tutor. There are hundreds of these small training organisations working in specialist niches, but not many of them are in Sally's league. Anyway, I was on this course and Sally and I got talking during a coffee break. I asked how she kept herself up-to-date with all the new developments in IT systems, computers, networks and so on. Her slides and course handbooks are superb, as you will see when you go on the course.

"Sally told me that one of the biggest risks in her line of business is falling behind her clients in IT systems. In her line of work, people who don't keep in touch with new techniques risk losing credibility with their customers. She reckons on attending eight to ten courses a year just to keep herself up to date. Well, knowing how much my place on Sally's course was costing, I said that IT training must take quite a chunk out of her income. Sally gave me a funny look. She told me that she wouldn't like it that way, so she arranges it that *they pay her*."

"You mean she actually gets paid for attending courses and learning new IT skills? How on earth does she manage that?" I asked.

"She's a training course auditor," Larry replied.

I didn't know there were such people, and Larry said that had been his reaction, too. Sally had said maybe there weren't but that didn't make it impossible. So she made it possible. She figured that if she could attend other people's training sessions then not only could she acquire the IT skills she needed for her own training work but she could also help the tutors to improve the content and presentation of their courses. Apparently, the way she works it is that she looks through her clients' course schedules and makes herself available at times when they're doing the sorts of courses she really needs to attend. She critically reviews a course and all its support documentation. As a result, they improve their image and win more repeat business, and Sally gets paid while developing her own IT skills. It's a fair deal, she reckons. Certainly, nobody resents what she is doing and they're always delighted with the help she gives them."

It's easy to see the logic after someone has made it make sense.

It's easy to see the logic behind a novel idea once someone else has made it make sense

"And another thing," Larry continued. "If there's anything in a course that Sally doesn't understand, they go over it together so that she, and anyone else who does the course in future, can get a really clear understanding."

"She sounds like a very clever lady," I said.

"I wouldn't know about that," Larry replied. "But she's certainly smart."

You don't have to be clever to act smart

I had asked for practical examples and, as usual, Larry had delivered the goods. I now understood how these two people had turned what would normally cost a lot into something that costs them nothing but is worth a great deal, both to themselves and to their customers. Larry had imagineered his opportunity as a book reviewer on the radio, and then used logic to extend it to include contributing to a prestigious management journal. In so doing he had reaped additional benefits from his interest in reading, rather than accepting buying the books as a necessary and unavoidable cost.

Imagineering can change costs into benefits

In Sally Cotterell's case she had turned a serious risk (the risk of becoming out of touch with technological developments) into a major career-development opportunity for herself and a valuable business benefit for her clients.

Turning risk into opportunity can mean a great deal for all concerned

It is now very clear to me that the principles of opportunity management can be applied to any kind of work. They can help you with your career, with your hobbies and other interests – with your whole life, in fact.

After Larry Farlow's introduction to the concept of turning risk into opportunity, I determined to make it *my* philosophy of life. I am always on the lookout for opportunities. Maybe I miss more unicorns than ever I harness. Maybe a more creative person would harness bigger and better specimens. But my unicorns are unique; they owe their very existence to me and they have repaid me many times over for the hours I spent imagineering them.

My unicorns are unique; they owe their very existence to me

I still refer to my notebook of ideas for recognising opportunities, for finding hidden opportunities and for creating new opportunities – after all these years it's rather a dog-eared little book. Before Larry set off in search of his new challenge, he helped me to fill in this page:

Subject: Towards new horizons

- Unicorn hunting is child's play.
- Nonsense is tomorrow's gateway to today's impossible dream.
- Imagination lives within us all; we should not let it die there.
- Chaotic thoughts are not necessarily idle thoughts.
- Ordinary people can have extraordinarily good ideas – imagine!
- Risk can magically become opportunity – you've got to believe it!
- New horizons are never discovered by following old roads.

Action: The future is an exciting place. Think about it – and harness the unicorn.

Summary

My notebook, full of Larry's aphorisms, is fine as a personal *aide-mémoire*; but for anyone new to the concepts of managing opportunity a summary, chapter by chapter, could be useful too. So here goes.

Chapter 1

For most people work, and indeed life generally, involves risks. There are risks in anything that is being changed, anything being done for the first time, anything being done a new way or by people unfamiliar with the work. Projects, assignments, organisation change, promotion, forming a new team – most people get involved in some or all of these from time to time; for many of us, it is the reason we are there. In short, all jobs involve risk, and the opportunities for things to go unexpectedly wrong are endless. Ignoring risks is a recipe for disaster: it's only a matter of time before one or more of the risks becomes reality and presents you with problems. Sorting out problems after they occur – reactive management – takes time, consumes money and effort, adds pressure. So most people would recognise the value of thinking ahead, of trying to anticipate problems and to head them off. That is risk management.

But no matter how hard we try, we will never be able to anticipate all possible risks. No amount of pondering will resolve all imponderables. Some of the unexpected things that throw us off course and off schedule are way outside our own control. One approach to coping with risk is simply to expect the unexpected and to hold sufficient time, money and resources in reserve, just in case. This entirely reactive approach is some-times called planned crisis management. The snag with the just-in-case philosophy is that it makes us less competitive. Wasted resources still have to be paid for; they pile additional costs on to the productive work we do, and so in practice hoarding away mountains of spare resource is rarely an option.

Jim Hallam's approach was to wait and see. When the unexpected setback occurred he would switch into crisis-management mode. All too often he would overload himself and his team members, work all hours to sort out as many of the problems as possible, let his company down by overspending the budget and eroding profitability, and let his customers down by delivering late.

So what are the alternatives?

Larry Farlow points out that managing risk is managing only one aspect of uncertainty. Any job that contains risk is likely also to be a source of opportunity, and we can manage opportunity too. Opportunities enable us to save work, to cut costs, to meet tighter schedules, to improve quality. And to enjoy life much more.

Unlike risks, the majority of opportunities, if ignored, go away. Therefore, reactive opportunity management is not the most productive strategy; we need a different approach, an approach based on taking the initiative *before* an opportunity arrives. Indeed, Larry suggests that unique opportunities have to be imagined before they can become real. So what Jim Hallam needs is time to think about opportunities; and yet, in his world of continual crisis management, productive thinking time is something Jim has squeezed out of his overloaded schedule.

Chapter 2

There are clear parallels between effective time management and successful opportunity management. Just like lost opportunity, lost time cannot be recovered. It is therefore worth considering the costs and benefits of everything that takes up our time, and not necessarily accepting other people's priorities, which may be based merely upon what is most urgent.

The persistent pursuit of perfection is the enemy of excellence. Perfection and excellence should not be confused: when there is insufficient time to do everything to the highest standard possible (and isn't that invariably the case at work?) it is the *outcomes* of work, as opposed to its *outputs*, that should drive our time-allocation decisions. Larry uses two tasks to illustrate this point to Jim. The first is a request for a report on furniture needs – Jim has to produce a report, but not at the expense of failing to meet a tender date for a major bid to a client. A hand-written memo is just good enough to obtain the furniture allocation Jim's people need; in contrast, the very best proposal document will be needed if Jim and his team are to win the contract competition.

Whereas risk management can help you reduce the cost, delay or other negative impacts of an unexpected and undesirable occurrence, opportunity management can also be a means of increasing the benefits associated with an activity or task. With risks and with opportunities you have more flexibility to shift priorities if you act early. Once you are up against the end stop as far as the time schedule is concerned, there is rarely a lot you can do to shift priorities, to alter the costs and to increase benefits.

Since most people perform best when doing things they enjoy, Larry Farlow recommends that Jim should take initiatives to raise the importance of some of the things he really enjoys doing. This, Larry says, is the essence of proactive opportunity management. It requires imagination and creativity, and therefore it is important to make time for creative thinking when you are not tired.

There were two key points that Jim needs to work on. First he has to stop striving for perfection in everything so that he can achieve excellence based on exceptionally high performance on the things that matter most. And second, he needs to think ahead and plan initiatives to head off risks and to find, create and exploit opportunities.

The first point was clear to Jim, and he had already begun applying it with the hand-written report on furniture needs. On the second point, the question still remained – how?

Chapter 3

Larry tells Jim about four distinctly different types of opportunities:

- Copycat opportunities
- Windfall opportunities
- Hidden opportunities
- Imagineered opportunities.

There may be other kinds of opportunities, too – for example opportunities that can only be realised by treating them as combinations of two or more of the above types.

Copying other people's initiatives is a very good way of keeping up with the pack. Those who believe success is the greater if they achieve it all by themselves often fail. Keeping in touch with trends in your own markets is important, and asking for help is a good way of reducing risks and finding opportunities.

You don't necessarily have to copy only the ideas of people who are doing work similar to your own. You can also look across to other organisations – a shopkeeper might learn from a hospital; a chemical processing plant from the legal professions – and find opportunities that none of your competitors is aware of.

Some people may have stumbled on an opportunity and become an overnight success. They were fortunate: they were in the right place at the right time. But such occurrences are rare; more often, those who end up with windfall opportunities do so because they take an active part in creating and managing their good fortune. There is no need to rely on luck to find you in the right place at the right time: if you know what you want, why not go where it is likely to be and at a time when it is most likely to be there?

So the first step in securing more windfall opportunities is to decide what kind of opportunities you want. Only then can you take the second step of working out where these opportunities are likely to be most plentiful and when you need to be there. If you are too slow off the mark, any windfall opportunities could get snapped up by someone else. And if no one seizes them early enough they are unlikely to keep: they go off. So step three is to exploit the opportunities you find. For example, you can use this largely reactive opportunity-management technique every time you visit another department, a customer or a supplier – but only if you have thought through what information you ought to be looking out for. Thinking well ahead is the key. Crisis managers rarely have time to think long term.

Hidden opportunities require a more proactive management approach. Larry Farlow suggests that the risky aspects of any job are the most likely to contain hidden opportunities. These are also the areas where people tend to switch into analytical mode, and in so doing they suppress their creativity.

Faced with the prospect of something going wrong, a natural reaction is to seek answers to the questions:

- How can we reduce the chances of this happening?
- How can we reduce the damage caused if it does happen?

These are sensible questions anyone ought to ask themselves when in a risky situation. But another approach is to ask:

● How could we turn this unexpected happening to our advantage?

Instead of trying to avert a disaster it may be possible to change something else so that what would have been an undesirable outcome now becomes a desirable one. There are many occasions when planning how you will deal with problems and being prepared for them is a more cost-effective strategy than trying to avoid problems altogether.

Imagineering, the source of the final category of opportunity, is an entirely creative process; it produces opportunities that would never have existed – for you or for anyone else – without you first imagining an attractive situation and then finding a way of making it come true – a way of harnessing the unicorn. And for that to happen you have to believe in the possibility of something you have never ever seen or heard of before.

There are barriers to overcome. Not least of these is the belief, held by many of us, that we are not creative. Tiredness forces us into such negative thoughts about our creativity; but there are also processes that can help us mobilise our imagineering capabilities. Jim Hallam needed to learn what these opportunity-management processes are and how to use them.

Chapter 4

Jim's approach to risk management was crude. It consisted of allocating some additional budget to those parts of the job that the team considered risky. The idea was that by mobilising extra resources his team might somehow be able to get things running according to plan. Larry Farlow was unimpressed. He said that when things don't go to plan you should use the plan to make decisions that change the future, and that means changing the detail of the plan so that your goals can still be met.

When estimating for work that contains risks, it is helpful to break your estimate into components:

- Well-defined and understood work. You can estimate this accurately based on past results. (It is advisable to use more than one method of estimating and to cross-check the results.)
- Ill-defined work. This includes allowance for interruptions and unexpected risks. (Rarely are all risks foreseeable at the outset.)
- Scrap and rework. If you have records of past performance in this respect, it makes sense to use them (although you may also need to set a target for improving efficiency).
- Foreseen risks. Here you need to plan the resources and time necessary to manage the risks you can foresee in the work.

The behaviour of people, the nature of the work, the environment (technical, social, commercial, political, and so on) in which the work is done – these can all be sources of risk, and not all of these risks are predictable.

Major risks can greatly alter the nature of a job, just as the opening or non-opening of a parachute can have a significant effect on the future of a paratrooper. For each major risk, it is wise to plan extra initiatives that can reduce the impact of the risk occurring or the likelihood of it doing so. The level of risk exposure is the product of the impact of the risk – the consequential loss or damage – and its probability. So, for example, a risk carrying a 10 per cent chance of putting you ten weeks behind schedule results in a one-week risk exposure, as does a 50 per cent chance of slipping two weeks. It's always worth brainstorming alternative mitigation measures and then deciding which to adopt.

When you have risk-mitigation options offering similar levels of exposure reduction at similar cost, it is generally preferable to choose the option that gives greatest reduction in impact, because this leaves you with a more predictable outcome. Some relatively minor risks may also deserve mitigation resources simply because of human perception; in particular, customers might expect to see you taking seriously their concerns.

Proactive initiatives can act as counter-measures to risk by reducing the impact or the probability (or both) of the risk occurring; however, rarely can every risk be mitigated fully, and some may be too costly to mitigate by counter-measures. The idea is to build in mitigation measures only to the extent that the cost of the counter-measures is less than the reduction in risk exposure. So, unless the residual risk exposure is negligible, you will also need a contingency plan – a plan of how you intend to react should the residual risk become reality. A good risk-management approach usually involves both counter-measures and contingency plans.

In a resource-limited situation (and who isn't?) you will need a means of setting priorities. For this you can use a risk-exposure map on which all major risks are plotted using as coordinates the levels of impact and probability. The idea, then, is to allocate risk-mitigation resources starting with the most serious risks and working your way down until you run out of resources. (But remember also to consider public perception, customer perception, and so on in situations where these factors may be relevant.)

Having made a plan for managing risks, it is essential to keep it under review: as your understanding of the situation improves so alternative strategies for mitigating risks more fully or at lower cost may become apparent. Some risks may prove to have been purely imaginary, and you may be able to release resources from unnecessary mitigation measures; other, initially un-imagined risks may become all too evident and require counter-measures for mitigation.

It takes time and effort to gain a reasonable understanding of the specific risks inherent in a job and of the global risks within the environment in which the work is to be carried out. In so doing, you will also acquire a much better appreciation of what is likely to happen as work proceeds and what sort of information will be needed to plan and manage the work properly.

Chapter 5

As you move from largely reactive, copycat management of opportunities to the more proactive strategies of turning risk into opportunity or of imagineering totally new opportunities, so you depend more and more upon the creativity of the people involved. Larry Farlow suggests to Jim that tiredness resulting from working long hours can be a real barrier to creativity. Error terror – fear of the consequences of making mistakes – also influences people to stick with what they understand rather than to seek new, imaginative solutions to problems. Creating a non-threatening environment, free from short-term time pressures, is a great help when you want to encourage a team to produce original ideas. Making the process fun is also important. And most of all, it is essential to shake off traditional thinking and analytical, critical behaviour.

For creativity to flourish we need to apply creative processes in a positive atmosphere. Everyone involved has to learn to value ideas that might not make immediate sense. (Indeed, if they do they are probably not original ideas.) Brainstorming and springboarding are just two of many processes that we can use to look at problems from new viewpoints and find new opportunities not evident when looking at the situation in familiar ways. Comments of the form *'That might work if . . .'* are generally more valuable at this stage than *'Yes but . . .'* criticisms. Things shouldn't be seen as either possible or impossible, but rather as possible or 'not possible yet'. In any case, even the silliest of suggestions from one person might spark off a really good idea from another, but this is unlikely to happen unless everyone lets their imagination run wild and every suggestion, no matter how zany, is valued and recorded. So we come to the idea of an opportunity logbook: a record of new ideas some of which may already have proven useful (the benefits of the opportunity have been realised at least once) and others which are yet to earn their colours, so to speak. In the end, of course, logic reduces the log of potential opportunities to a shortlist that you are able to exploit immediately.

Separating in time the processes of idea generation and idea analysis makes it easier to manage the environment, and particularly the intellectual atmosphere, within which each process is carried out. It is also unreasonable to ask people to concentrate on the analytical job of managing risks and to expect them at the same time to find, recognise and create opportunities. For that reason, Larry Farlow recommends that Jim should keep both a risk register and an opportunity log but that he should not try to deal with the two together. We need mainly analytical process for risk management, but a lot more creative thinking when considering opportunity.

Chapter 6

There is much to be gained from finding and exploiting opportunities within the activities of everyday work – the business-as-usual part of the job as well as change initiatives, projects and special assignments. If Larry is right and most of the opportunities are to be found in the high-risk parts of the job, then the risk register would seem to be a good starting point.

For each major risk, the risk register shows the intended mitigation counter-measures, the costs and benefits anticipated, and any residual risk and the contingency plans for dealing with it should the need arise. Initially, the register will contain many risks; the intention is, as work proceeds, to avoid, avert or otherwise mitigate these. The opportunity log, in contrast, starts empty, the intention being to fill it with opportunities that save time and money or provide additional benefits to the organis-ation, to its staff, to its customers or to its key suppliers. The idea, then, is that as work proceeds you empty the risk register and fill up the opportunity log.

It sounds simple enough; but, for people such as Jim's team who are not used to mobilising their creativity, there is nothing like getting a bit of help from a skilled facilitator. The team members concentrate on the task at hand, while the facilitator focuses on managing the creative process.

Risk management and opportunity management are not things that you add on to a basic plan: they need to be integrated into the plan. Indeed, your overall strategy – the general approach you decide to take on any high-risk work – is best chosen not in isolation but only after considering the risks and opportunities inherent in each of the approaches available to you. It is generally unwise to compare options solely on an assessment of their predicted 'if all goes well' outcomes, so you really need rough-order-of-magnitude estimates and top-level risk assessments for each option rather than a very detailed analysis of a single option that might turn out to be far from optimal when risk and opportunity are taken into account.

For high-risk work, task-based plans are rarely the most useful starting point. You are unlikely to know at the outset exactly what you need to do in the later stages of the work, and to succeed you will need to take advantage of everything you learn as the work proceeds. You can't do this if you commit yourself to specific tasks at the outset. For this reason, it is usually better to make plans that are based on milestones which are genuine elements of achievement. Each milestone will eventually need its own activity plan, but you will decide on the activities when your understanding is sufficient to allow you to make a meaningful plan, and not before. Pretending from the outset that you know the best way of doing something when in truth your understanding is quite inadequate is a sure way of building unnecessary risk into your work.

With increased dependence on teamwork, *everyone* needs to understand the goal and to commit themselves to the plan for achieving it. Another advantage of milestone-based planning is that the plans are so simple that everyone involved in the work can understand them.

Jim is worried that all of the initiatives for managing risk will extend his work schedule; he needs to *save* time, but everything Larry is suggesting appears to be extending the schedule. Larry is insistent, however, that the cost and time necessary for counter-measures work must be included in the baseline plan for the job. Counter-measures are things you intend doing in order to make the outcome more predictable and the work more manageable: without doubt they *will* consume resources.

Larry's solution is to cut the costs and timescales in the baseline estimate – but not to do so arbitrarily. He suggests setting opportunity-management targets – commitments to improving efficiency and effectiveness (mainly the latter). These savings need to be part of the plan, and the areas with greatest potential for opportunity are usually the high-risk aspects of the job. Strategies for finding and making the savings are, of course, based on the four types of opportunities, while the risk register and the opportunity log are the means of integrating the opportunity-management targets into the plan: the starting point for harnessing the unicorn and turning risk into opportunity.

Chapter 7

Before running the risk-management workshop, Larry gives the team a warm-up exercise. Although it is only a game, the team members soon find themselves engrossed in the challenge, and when the time comes to turn their attention to finding opportunities in their real work they are already familiar with the process. What they had not considered, however, were the criteria for success; consequently, the options they choose are not optimum. But with facilitation support, they are soon able to produce a sound risk-management strategy for the mock exercise, and that fuels their motivation so that in tackling the real work they are able to consider a range of options and to choose an approach based not simply on the 'if-all-goes-well' outcome. Not only do they save money, but their counter-measures initiatives give a significant forecast schedule saving.

It is essential to hold periodic reviews of the risk-management measures planned for later stages of the work, so that you can benefit fully from everything you learn while doing the earlier work. And in any case, as the team on a job grows in maturity they can often achieve improved results even if the information available has not changed significantly.

Opportunity workshops are often more effective when carried out away from the normal working environment. They also tend to benefit from a warm-up activity to get everyone into a positive '*can do*' frame of mind.

You can structure an opportunity workshop around the four opportunity types, choosing processes that suit the level of creativity involved. This has the advantage that the team works its way up from mainly reactive, copycat ideas through windfalls and hidden opportunities to imagineered ones, rather than trying to go straight into creative processes that many people find quite difficult at first.

When looking for copycat opportunities, simple checklists can prompt answers to questions such as:

- Whom could we copy?
- What other markets might have useful parallels with our own?

Windfalls are also easier to find if you give some forethought to them. It's easier to spot something if you know what you are looking for, and that in turn makes it easier to decide where and when you should be looking.

The risk register is a good place to look when hunting hidden opportunities. Again, knowing what types of opportunities you are looking for is a great help. For example, when you need to find time-saving opportunities, it's always worth looking closely at those aspects of the job that appear to carry the greatest schedule risks.

Finally to imagineering. Here perhaps the greatest barrier to be overcome is people's belief that they are not creative or that they don't know how to mobilise their creativity. Every child knows how to think imaginatively, to believe in the not yet possible, to play. And anything you wish can be used to trigger creative ideas. Larry Farlow used newspaper cuttings. The unpredictability of a novel and untried process might be a disadvantage in analytical work, but it is a positive advantage when you want to mobilise the creativity of a team. For this reason, it even helps if you change the trigger mechanism periodically, rather than risking getting into a rut by using the same process over and over again.

It isn't necessary to find all the opportunities you need right at the outset. Indeed, apart from on very short-term tasks this is hardly likely to prove possible. What you do need, however, is to find *some* opportunities – sufficient to convince team members that they will be able to find and create all the opportunity they need as the work proceeds. Creative opportunities are dependent on belief as well as commitment

As work proceeds, unexpected outcomes will inevitably appear. To treat them automatically as failures is a mistake. They may be potential problems but they might also be hidden opportunities. (Some opportunities appear initially to be terrifying monsters, but if treated as opportunities they can sometimes prove to be extremely helpful.)

Keeping the opportunity log visible ensures that everyone in the team can see the target and see what progress has been made towards achieving it. Individual opportunity-management achievements can be extremely motivating and should be a cause of team celebration. Similarly, it is important not to hide setbacks. As Larry Farlow put it, a high-profile problem is preferable to damage below the water line; it provides everyone with the challenge of seeking a creative solution. And even if things go terribly wrong, hiding failures means throwing away the opportunity to learn and to avoid similar problems in the future.

But learning – something that is central to opportunity management – should not be restricted to the areas where things go badly. Learning from success is also important. When things go exceptionally well, you need to find out why. What did people do differently this time? Learning from success is the key to becoming even more successful; it is altogether too good an opportunity to miss.

Chapter 8

A strategy for managing opportunity need not – indeed should not – be limited to the working hours of your life. Life itself is a unique experience for each one of us – as far as we know. Our lives need not be simply a series of accidents over which we have no control. We can manage the risks of everyday life, and we can, if we wish, also do a lot to find, create and manage opportunities in life outside work. If you want to get to somewhere new, remember, the old roads cannot take you there. You need a vision of what you would like your life to contain, and then you need to make a simple plan that incorporates opportunity-management initiatives.

Other people's good fortune may be just that. Or it may be that they are doing something constructive, either intuitively or by prior planning, to deserve their luck. If you are naturally intuitive, you may be used to having lots of good luck. But if, like Jim Hallam, you haven't been getting all the luck you need by relying on your intuition, why not try applying the principles of opportunity management outlined in this book? Copy the smart guys. Be in the right place at the right time to benefit from windfall opportunities. Turn some of life's most threatening risks into opportunities for increased success and happiness.

And believe in yourself and your imagineering ability: harness the unicorn.